Allan King

filmmaker

TORONTO INTERNATIONAL FILM FESTIVAL

in conjunction with

INDIANA UNIVERSITY PRESS
Bloomington and Indianapolis

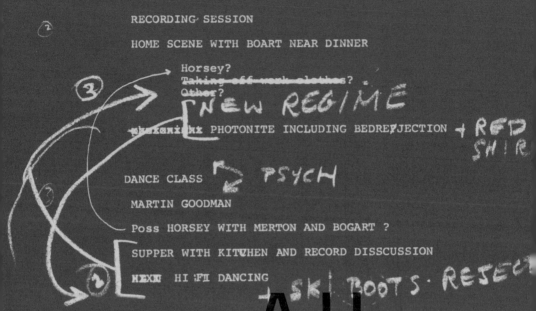

HOUSEWORK

RECORDING SESSION

HOME SCENE WITH BOART NEAR DINNER

Horsey?
~~Taking off work clothes~~?
Other?

NEW REGIME

~~overnight~~ PHOTONITE INCLUDING BEDREFLECTION + RED SHIR

DANCE CLASS **PSYCH**

MARTIN GOODMAN

Poss HORSEY WITH MERTON AND BOGART ?

SUPPER WITH KITCHEN AND RECORD DISSCUSSION

~~NEXT~~ HI :FI DANCING **SKI BOOTS. REJECT**

~~PARTY MONTAGE (III SHOTS)~~

TENDERNESS **By 1 SELF ?**

Allan

King

*for George

with my
great
gratitude

fondly Ana*

filmmaker

Edited by Seth Feldman

The Toronto International Film Festival gratefully acknowledges the support of The Canada Council for the Arts for publication of this book.

The Canada Council | Le Conseil des Arts
for the Arts | du Canada

Toronto International Film Festival Group
2 Carlton Street, Suite 1600, Toronto, Ontario, M5B 1J3 Canada

The Toronto International Film Festival Group is a charitable, cultural and educational organization dedicated to celebrating excellence in film and the moving image.

First edition

National Library of Canada Cataloguing in Publication Data

Main entry under title:
Allan King : filmmaker / edited by Seth Feldman

Includes bibliographical references.
ISBN 0-9689132-1-0

1. King, Allan, 1930–   –Criticism and interpretation.
I. Feldman, Seth, 1948–   II. Toronto International Film Festival.
PN1998.3.K55A44 2002   792'.023'092   C2002-903045-5

The Canadian Retrospective programmed at
the 2002 Toronto International Film Festival
is generously sponsored by

Distributed in Canada by Wilfrid Laurier Press
Website: wlupress.wlu.ca

Distributed outside Canada by Indiana University Press
Website: iupress.indiana.edu

Cover and text design: Gordon Robertson
Front cover image: *Warrendale*

Printed in Canada

for Renate

Contents

(opposite) Richard Leiterman and Allan King on the set of *Who Has Seen the Wind*
National Archives of Canada / PA212196

Preface

There are few Canadian filmmakers whose impact has been central to the medium, but Allan King is unquestionably one of them. His contribution to the documentary form, most notably that strand known as *cinema vérité*, is second to none. *Warrendale* and *A Married Couple* are two of the most important documentaries ever made and are acknowledged as such by critics and experts around the world.

But Allan King has given much more to Canadian cinema than those two films justly celebrated films. His work includes some of the key short documentaries made in this country (*Skidrow, Rickshaw*). He has directed a number of exceptionally fine television dramas for the Canadian Broadcasting Corporation (*Maria, Red Emma* and *Baptizing*) and one of the true classics of our fictional cinema (*Who Has Seen the Wind*). His documentary work subsequent to *Warrendale* and *A Married Couple* showed that he had lost none of his touch for socially explosive issues. *Who's in Charge?* was one of the most controversial and incendiary documentaries that the CBC ever showed.

Allan King has had an extraordinary career, but he is much more than a filmmaker plying his craft. In the seventies he was an essential member of the Council of Canadian Filmmakers, a group lobbying to place a distinctively Canadian stamp on our film and television industry. He supported, among other innovations, a universal pay television system from which revenues would be taken and ploughed back into the Canadian system (a battle that was not won). For many years he was president of the Director's Guild of Canada, working to get a better deal for native-born talent.

Allan King is a nationalist who fervently believes in a Canadian cinema, but he is also a man who has never been afraid of working in the international arena. As a young filmmaker he rapidly outgrew his native Vancouver and moved to Europe, where he chose subject matter that took him around the world. For years he had an office in London, England, and his last film was shot in Estonia.

What makes him distinctively Canadian is his endless fascination with questions of community. From the multinational exiles in *Running Away Backwards* through *Warrendale, Come On Children, Who's in Charge?, Who Has Seen the Wind* and right up to his most recent work, *The Dragon's Egg*, King has probed and examined this concept with singular passion and insight.

We are delighted to present a retrospective of Allan King's work at this year's Toronto International Film Festival. This book, which includes critical articles and an interview with the filmmaker, has been produced as a companion volume to the film series, and offers readers insights into the remarkable and continuing achievement of one of Canada's most provocative filmmakers.

Piers Handling
Director, Toronto International Film Festival
July 2002, Toronto

Seth Feldman

Paradise and Its Discontents

An Introduction to Allan King

Cinéma-vérité, the sub-genre of documentary filmmaking for which Allan King is best known, is one of those useful but elusive concepts chequering the landscape of cinema's history and thought. Like the terms "Hollywood" or "experimental cinema," everybody knows what "*cinéma-vérité*" means, but what everybody knows is slightly, or radically, different. The term itself was coined by the film historian Georges Sadoul in reference to Jean Rouch and Edgar Morin's 1960 film, *Chronique d'un été*.[1] Rouch and Morin used equipment that was newly available at the time, 16mm cameras synchronized to portable tape recorders, to interview selected Parisians on their various states of mind. The footage was edited together as a series of long uninterrupted takes. Its conclusions are open-ended—as Rouch and Morin, interviewing each other at the end of the film, acknowledge. The experiment was, they say, shrugging, a partial success.

Today, at least in the French-speaking world, *Chronique d'un été* would be called *cinéma direct*. The term "direct cinema" was used by Robert Drew to describe an entirely different, though contemporaneous, use of the same equipment in a series of made-for-television documentaries that Drew produced for Time-Life, beginning in 1960. Most English-speaking writers would now call these films *cinéma-vérité*. Each of the Time-Life films was a tightly edited story spun out of events that promised a certain degree of dramatic tension. Who will win the Wisconsin primary? Will a condemned man be saved from the electric chair? Will a very young Jane Fonda make it on Broadway? Unlike Rouch and Morin, the filmmakers Drew employed for his series—Richard Leacock, D. A. Pennebaker, the Maysles brothers and others—seldom appeared in their own films or interviewed their subjects on camera. They were, or so they claimed, mere flies on the wall as the action unfolded around them. The grand illusion created was that the stories told themselves.

In 1963, many of the French and American practitioners of this new form of documentary met in Lyon to air their stylistic and semantic differences.[2] Already, though, a third trend was emerging. It seemed that the tools of *cinéma-vérité* worked equally well to make fiction films. In France, Jean-Luc Godard shot his films quickly in the streets, mixing actors and non-actors, occasionally stopping the action to interview his characters. In the United States, John Cassavetes used his handheld camera to shoot, in single takes, long improvisational sequences by his actors. Nor were these isolated examples. By the mid-1960s there was a rising tide of gritty feature films that were to a greater or lesser degree indistinguishable from the *cinéma-vérité* and direct-cinema documentaries. Lest this irony be lost on anyone, Jim McBride and Kit Carson made *David Holzman's Diary* (1967), the first of many fictional films deliberately composed around *cinéma-vérité* clichés.[3]

The twin paradoxes of ostensibly objective documentaries requiring stylistic decisions and the concern that those decisions might subvert documentary itself are not bad entry points into the world of Allan King. Before, during and after the *cinéma-vérité* conundrums, King's films deftly navigated these pitfalls and contradictions. His work begins with his personal discovery of the talking-head interview, and is full of the kind of face-to-face encounters that characterized the French style. King has pointed his camera at everyone from world leaders to stoned hippies and captured a remarkable record of who they are and what they think they are doing. Like the Americans, King has had a long and distinguished career of presenting what he, in his own contribution to the semantic soup, once called "actuality dramas." Films like *Warrendale* (1966), *A Married*

Couple (1969) and *Who's in Charge?* (1983) evoked strong responses from broadcasters, critics and audiences. Since then, and with equal success, King has directed a long list of television dramas and feature films that owe much to the practised eye and the even more practised people skills of a *cinéma-vérité* filmmaker. Few filmmakers have as much to say in their documentaries about dramatic narrative and in their dramas about documentary style.

Warrendale

King was well placed to develop his own approach to both documentary and fiction filmmaking. He was there at several beginnings: the beginning of Canadian television; the introduction of the first synch sound cameras; the advent of *cinéma-vérité* in its various manifestations; Canada's golden age of anthology drama; the birth of the Canadian feature film industry; and even the establishment of a mature Canadian industry built to serve as a branch plant for American television. King displayed an acute consciousness of these moments and the opportunities they afforded. Within Canadian cinema, he has been something of a visionary. As often as not, he has had to wait for the industry to catch up to him.

Amid the many exaggerated reports of the death of the author (and his cinematic cousin, the *auteur*), King has, in the best of his films, advanced a single, coherent perspective. He has his motifs, his cast of characters and the threads that link them. His films, for instance, are often set in either utopian or dystopian landscapes. When we are in some sort of paradise, King, like Thomas More in the original *Utopia*, is often cagey about approving of the place. His utopians may be genuinely deserving—usually artists, or at least people who are trying to take the avant-garde life seriously—or they may be poseurs, who turn a perfect little world into its opposite. Ironically, the sadder, dystopian settings, thanks to the people in them, may turn out to offer a more realistic expectation of sanctuary and happiness than do the paradises.

The rules by which these plots unfold are strictly existential. Like so many of his generation, growing up in the intellectual shadow of Sartre, Camus or even Bergman, King believes that we cannot be or mean any more than our *actions*. Life is not what we say it is but how we live it. As he told the *Globe and Mail* in 1998: "At root, I think my films are about why it is that we have such difficulty doing what we say we want to do."[4] Choice, in King's films, is a terrible burden and at the same time a gift of inestimable value. King genuinely values the people he films as they work to make and live with their choices. He is obsessively non-judgmental regarding their final decisions (for judgment, in a world where there is no grand scheme of things, is meaningful only to the judge). His documentaries and dramas avoid ideologies and polemics. They tend to be populated by individuals who refuse to be categorized.

From the beginning, the quiet intimacy with which King framed his subjects generated considerable discomfort in many of his viewers and a few of those who commissioned his work. Rejecting superficial scenarios of victims and villains has, in some circles, made him a political pariah. At the same time, he is not an iconoclast for the sake of iconoclasm; he has made films in which institutions are as valued as individuals. Unashamedly entrepreneurial, he has also dedicated years of his life to the collective development of a national cinema. What has distinguished him from those who have not achieved as much is perhaps the deliberation with which he undertakes his work. King is a thinker and researcher who usually digests a small library before beginning work on a major film. His thoughtfulness, combined with the elusive nature of *cinéma-vérité* and the make-it-up-as-you-go-along aesthetic that sheer necessity has imposed upon much of Canadian filmmaking, has resulted in films as varied and challenging as the times in which they were made.

Beginnings

The origins of King's contemplative approach are, like the origins of so much else in Canadian culture, at least partly geographic. As a native of Vancouver, he was (according to the stereotype) born to be laid-back. This clichéd view of Vancouverites' style has much to do with their decidedly un-Canadian lack of environmental tribulation. This is not the bone-chilling tundra, the muggy, mosquito-infested bush or the windswept prairie. While the rest of Canada endures its grim nation-building struggle against the elements, Vancouver is warmed by Pacific currents that cause the tulips to bloom in February. The Vancouver of popular imagination—a pristine city, surrounded by snow-capped peaks—bears an all but embarrassing resemblance to Hollywood's Shangri-La. And like Shangri-La, the Vancouver of King's childhood existed in splendid isolation, tenuously linked to Central Canada by a four-day train ride, a rickety air service and, when it was passable, a three-thousand-mile country road.

Born in the first months of the Great Depression, Allan Winton grew up in a pre-lapsarian landscape in which the threat of being booted out of Eden was never far from anyone's mind. As King remembers it, in bourgeois Vancouver the consequences of failure could be measured by clearly marked physical borders:

> As the depression struck, we fell—moving almost every year,
> but never crossing the imaginary line marked by Cambie Street
> to the east of Kerrisdale, much less that of the Main Street
> boundary—which was like that of a ghetto, come to think of it.
> East of Main was where the working class lived.[5]

The Wintons' fall was harder and more painful than most. Allan's father, a travelling salesman, was an alcoholic whose drinking cost him his job and, after much turmoil, his marriage. The young Allan and his sister were forced to live with other families while their mother struggled with her financial and emotional crises. At length she remarried and, as was the custom at the time, the children took their new father's surname: hence, Allan Winton King, a name he has always regarded with some ambivalence.

Although King would see his birth father only once more during his lifetime, his films would be populated by fathers, father figures, lost and forgotten old men.

Despite his childhood traumas, King did well in school, working hard for the teachers who took an interest in him and taking on responsibility from an early age. At fifteen, he began working summers in logging camps and was eventually entrusted, by much older men, with the job of union representative. His friends were other smart and hardworking kids, many of them inclined toward the arts. As King writes elsewhere in this volume, one of those friends, Stan Fox, led him into an avocation as an impresario at the Vancouver Film Society, and, after other adventures, into filmmaking itself at the CBC's new Vancouver television station, CBUT.

Skidrow (1956), King's first film, was a portrait of derelict and homeless men. It was also an early contribution to a wave of made-for-television documentaries that would later (at least in Central Canada) be called "the West Coast School." King, though, was not thinking of joining or starting a movement; his interest was in pursuing the unfinished business of his childhood geography by crossing over to the long-feared wrong side of the tracks. The material he found there became, as Robert Russell described it, "a complete and totally satisfying portrait of a timeless world,"[6] *Skidrow* was also, in a small, personal way, an experiment with the early techniques of cinema itself.

> Bits of it rank with Chaplin: the mimed party in the flophouse, the panhandler at work in the street, the alley-brawl of a sodden drunk and his even more unfortunate rival. These wordless but eloquent illustrations of the elements of life use techniques of the earliest days of silent film: the camera is plunked squarely, inflexibly before the action. Allan King was beginning at the beginning.[7]

The film is marked by a dynamic tension between two distinct modes of presenting its subject. Most of it consists of silent images commented upon by Arthur Hives reading Ben Maartman's script. Besides being the social worker who guided King through the derelict streets, Maartman was also a pub-

Skidrow

lished writer. The polished language he uses is descended from the fiction and, even more, the theatre of the Great Depression. It is a tough-talking howl of despair, identifying while also accepting the details of being poor and, to the respectable world, invisible. Like the voice-over narrations that had been part of documentary for a quarter of a century, this lament dominates and shapes the images beneath it.

Skidrow also features short synchronized sound interviews with the men who are the subjects of the film. The use of synch sound in documentary did not begin with *Skidrow*; newsreels had, since the late 1920s, included short segments of synchronized speech, usually by celebrities or heads of state. By 1956, though, thanks to the changing technology of television news-gathering, location sound was becoming more prevalent and more democratic. *Skidrow* spoke to this new expectation that anyone might be given a voice. Each time one of the men speaks, it is a jolt, an abrupt change in the film's tone. Their words are far simpler than the literary narration, their speech softer than Maartman's voice of doom. Neither angry nor sarcastic, they quietly answer questions about their daily existence. Even more striking is the way they describe, albeit with some prompting, their past lives. No longer the victims of fate, much less cartoonish hoboes, they are simply men looking the viewer in the eye. It is not *cinéma-vérité*, not yet. But these eye-to-camera monologues are far more than sound bites. The synch sound segments in *Skidrow* demonstrate the power of letting people tell their own stories in their own words, and give some hint of the profound effect that technique would have on King's work—and on documentary as a whole.

Knowing full well that his own father could be sitting on some similar street, King leaves us with a work that focuses not on the alcoholics' misery but on the fact that they had a choice. The four other films King made for CBUT films are also autobiographical in various ways and they too are remarkably blunt in framing their subjects' difficulties as nothing more or less than the consequences of their actions. *The Yukoners* (1956), his second film, begins in much the same way as Colin Low's much better known NFB production *City of Gold* (1957). Both introduce us to what was left in the 1950s of the 1897 Klondike gold rush. But while the NFB production quickly cuts to stills of the rollicking old days, King stays with the aged prospectors themselves, showing them as the old men they have become, no longer part of the Klondike myth. They stayed behind, panning the dwindling supply of gold left on their tiny claims. A modern mining industry has grown up around them, but they live alone in primitive cabins, keeping their independence as long as they can until, inevitably, they are forced to move to the Dawson City old age home for their few remaining days.

Portrait of a Harbour and *Gyppo Loggers* (both 1957) take a similar approach to King's familiar stomping grounds, Vancouver and the backwoods logging camps. Neither, though, is as complex as *The Pemberton Valley* (1958), the last of King's CBUT films. King flew into the stunningly beautiful, then isolated British Columbia locale. His plan was to shoot his own version of Georges Rouquier's *Farrebique* (1946), the story of an extended family's bond with the land. Jack Long's pastoral images and Robert Turner's music are in harmony with that goal; King's eye and George Robertson's narration go in other directions. Far from the "thoroughly static view of a thoroughly static valley"[8] that Guy Coté would later call it, the film has an edgy, dark undertone. We learn that the farmer King has chosen to document is a recent immigrant and that he has had a difficult time being accepted by the valley's other inhabitants. His family includes a number of foster children, most of whom are adjusting to life on the farm, one of whom has an especially dark past. No sooner does the farm family plant their potatoes than the film abruptly cuts to the nearby native reserve, a location that has very little to do with anyone's idea of Shangri-La. There, the inhabitants stoically accept their unemployment, their second-class status and the mixed-blood children local whites leave behind. On Victoria Day, the men ride in a manic horse race through the reserve's muddy streets. This part of the film focuses on a young native man who comes to the conclusion that, if his life is to mean anything, he must leave his dead-end community behind.

King, at this juncture, came to something like the same conclusion about his own life. In 1958, he resigned from CBUT, quitting the last salaried job he ever would hold. Two years and five films into his career, he was chafing at the CBUT's bureaucracy. He was also not willing to spend a career documenting life in British Columbia. But most important, King now had a place to go. His first wife's sister and her husband, the painter Rolph Blakstad, were living in an expatriate community on Ibiza. That Spanish island became King's paradise away from home. It was hotter than Vancouver in both climate and temperament, and the artists that he met there inspired in him a lifelong interest in the avant-garde and the creative personality. They would also supply him with a second education.

> For me the invaluable reward was the realization of who I was. With all the talk, the drink, taking part in this multi-national and cultural circus, I was able to incorporate the differences between the cultures in which my friends and I grew up; how they shaped us and gave us, each and every one, our unique perspectives. This sense, which is the reward for enduring the wrenching pain of adolescence, the terror of cutting loose from dependency, was the gelling of identity and all the values that go with it. It is the source of one's voice; without it one cannot speak, with it one may.[9]

King's plan was to support himself on Ibiza by making films for the CBC's documentary program, *Close-up*. When the Franco government, dark masters of this sunny isle, made it difficult for him to work there, he established a second European base in London. King (a.k.a. Allan King Associates) filmed Berber tribesman in the mountains of Morocco and shot footage of Saigon between the French and American Vietnam wars. Along with Blakstad, whom he trained as a cameraman, King began travelling the globe, sending a series of short documentaries home to far-off Canada. *Where Will They Go?* (1959) dealt with the unwilling internees in an Austrian refugee camp. *Bullfight* (1960) contrasted romantic echoes of Hemingway's *Death in the Afternoon* with the camera's unblinking record of the sad and brutal business of killing an imprisoned animal.

The most successful of King's globe-trotting *Close-up* films was *Rickshaw* (1960). Shot on the streets of Calcutta, as wrong as any side of the tracks can get, the film introduces us to a worn-out middle-aged pedicab puller in

Rickshaw

the last days of his job. George Robertson's narration tells us that the man has never had more than the absolute minimum needed to sustain his non-stop barefoot running through the hot city streets. He has spent years separated from his family in his home village. When we find him, he is about to be released from the killing routine of his job, though only at the price of passing it on to his teenage son. The boy arrives at the train station, runs beside his father for a day and then takes up the handles to pull his father on a first and last rickshaw ride. That ride ends at the train station where the old man goes home, having nothing to show for his years in Calcutta.

Rickshaw is so completely despairing that it is tempting to escape its implications by seeing it as either polemic or allegory. Neither reading works. Nowhere in its narration does the film demand justice for pedicab operators, blame anyone for this man's situation or offer the slightest idea how his life might be made easier. The compelling reality of what the camera finds prevents us from looking beyond this one man in this one place. What the film does best it does by presenting the simple fact that King has somehow found the rickshaw puller and is, against all odds, telling his story. To suggest that what we are seeing is a rhetorical argument or some sort of parable would be to undermine and lessen the power of the film's existential poetry.

Close-up also hired King to direct a series of interviews with some of the foremost creative and political personalities of the day: Orson Welles, Anthony Eden, Nehru and Peter Sellers among many others. He filmed Charles de Gaulle's ministers hovering about de Gaulle's barely metaphorical throne. In 1967, the CBC entrusted King with the task of recording the Queen's Canadian Centennial message (he directed Her Majesty through eight takes). His portraits of creative artists—the actor Christopher Plummer, the sculptor Josef Drenters, the ballerina Lynn Seymour—led Allan King Associates into a co-production agreement with the CBC, the BBC, National Education Television (now PBS) and Bayerische Rundfunk to produce twelve one-hour documentaries under the title *Creative Persons* (1968–69).

In the 1960s, the documentary portrait was not only King's stock in trade but also an important part of his own thinking about the films he made. He may have needed to see the world in the largest possible context, but he was rapidly coming to the conclusion that the way he was going to see it as a documentary filmmaker was in eye-level contact with individual subjects. He wrote in 1966:

> My only interest in film making is in capturing the character of the individual being filmed. Though ideas, politics and social questions interest me, I have a strong distrust of intellectual analysis, yet cannot leave it alone. All positions seem vulnerable and therefore unacceptable as positions to be taken up in any firm way. . . . Philosophically I seem to be caught in a sort of Hegelianism; it is not possible to know the truth unless you know the whole of reality and that is not humanly possible. Yet one wishes to pursue the truth.[10]

Nowhere was this philosophical dilemma more evident than in *A Matter of Pride* (1961), one of the most powerful films King made for *Close-up* in the early 1960s. The truth he wished to pursue was the experience of unemployment in his own rich country. King chose to cover the issue by focusing on the Exelbys, a Hamilton family. Mr. Exelby, a salesman, had lost his job some months before. The family's lower-middle-class life has been disintegrating, sliding toward desperation. Most of this is conveyed in long interviews, two of which are with Mrs. Exelby, shot in tight close-up, her make-up intact and her pearls still neatly draped around her neck. In both interviews, she cries (as does her husband, almost imperceptibly, in his interview). These public displays of emotion sparked an internal debate at the CBC as to whether the show could be aired. When it was broadcast, it provoked a wave of audience response, articles in the press and some hounding of the Exelbys themselves. The outcry went as far as Parliament, where the minister of labour rose to claim that King had fabricated the family's suffering and had—because he paid a fee to his subjects—"bought" their tears. The CBC, well stocked with government appointees, refused to rebut the public criticism and was further cowed when the film's producers and King were summoned to Ottawa for a stern dressing-down.

Dramatic Experiments

Not particularly humbled by this chastisement, King turned in an entirely different direction. He had, from the time of the CBUT documentaries, improvised short staged scenes in his work. As early as *Skidrow*, he had "rehearsed" some of the interview material with the men in the film and in *Rickshaw*, he had asked the characters to "perform" those aspects of their daily lives that he needed for the film. Now, King took another step toward drama, a television half-hour entitled *Dreams* (1962) for the CBC series, *Quest*. The film is about a young couple living together in Toronto. He is an aspiring painter who is growing increasingly restless, and she is becoming worried about his leaving. Within this context, the rules for the film's production tested the boundary between documentary and drama.

> The couple were playing themselves, there were no interviews but the action was directed—as in *Rickshaw*. I discovered he was going to leave her but hadn't told her, that she knew but hadn't spoken to him and spent a day with each separately, exploring their feelings about the expected event, asked if he wished to tell her about it and if she wanted to respond: invited them to "play the scene" if you will. Is it a documentary? Is it a drama? These names are artifices and when pressed rather meaningless.[11]

In 1962, King resumed his experimentation with the fictional uses of a *cinéma-vérité* style. He did so in a series of films, the first of which was his adaptation of the "Field Day" scene from the Living Theatre's London production of Kenneth Brown's play *The Brig*. Set in a Marine Corps prison, the play was brutally realistic and King had his longtime cinematographer, Richard Leiterman, shoot the scene in three takes from on stage, amid the actors. The finished work is largely composed of close-ups of the faces of both the guards and the prisoners as they go through a hyperkinetic cleaning of the jail cell, while maintaining parade-ground discipline. Interestingly enough, King's other principal cinematographer of the period, William Brayne, edited the work. The resulting film—used in a CBC current affairs documentary entitled *The Peacemakers* (1963) and again on

Quest—is an intense twelve minutes in which it is easy to forget that we are watching a play or actors.[12]

King's second, more ambitious experiment was with what might be called observational drama. After spending some time in Lagos, he commissioned *Joshua: A Nigerian Portrait* (1963) from Wole Soyinka, an emerging African dramatist whose work had already been produced on the London stage. The film portrays a young rent collector attempting to balance the traditional extended family life of his rural village with his more complicated transactions in the wider society of newly post-colonial Lagos. Its cast is made up of non-actors, many of whom who are doing pretty much what they usually do in their daily lives. Soyinka's script contained little dialogue and much of what we hear in the film was improvised by the writer and King during the shoot. Looking at the film, a viewer finds it often difficult to tell who is acting and who is simply going about his or her business. King regards the film as a collaboration; as such, it has a place in post-colonial African literature, and perhaps with the African films that were to appear shortly thereafter.

In 1964, King made two dramatic films with similar themes, both from scripts by Robert Goldston and both commissioned by Douglas Leiterman, the executive producer of CBC's *Document* series. *Bjorn's Inferno* tells the story of the New York poet Bjorn Halverson, an Ibiza returnee who plays himself, or at least some imagined version of himself. The poet must decide whether to trade in his bohemian lifestyle for a job as a computer operator in an insurance company. His internal debate is sufficiently heartfelt to crack open the conventions of film narrative. The film is interrupted with silent film titles and an overblown music score. Our poet is tempted to take the job by a loquacious *bon vivant* who is either the Devil or his own imaginative construct, extrapolated from an odd-looking man he spotted on the subway (he was, in reality, Barry Simmons, another of King's former Ibiza neighbours). There is a long sequence in which Bjorn takes his family through a deserted theme park, instantly dressing in a series of costumes to act out the park's various sub-themes. In contrast to the *cinéma-vérité* style of King's first three dramatic films, *Bjorn's Inferno* goes all out in an attempt to document a poet's life from inside his own head. A generous reading of its achievement would place it in the context of contemporaneous films like

Shooting *Running Away Backwards*

Richard Lester's *A Hard Day's Night* (1964), in which the Beatles are given similar licence to change reality in accordance with their perception of it.

King's second drama of 1964, *Running Away Backwards*, was about people who were living a kind of "Bjorn's Paradiso." Set on Ibiza, the film revolves around and is entirely acted by the island's expatriate community. It is a remarkable period piece, documenting the twilight of the traditional expatriate bohemia—and simultaneously, the last moments of a North American culture so stifling as to leave no alternative but flight. The protagonist of *Running Away Backwards* is a loquacious writer who seems to actually write from time to time, while spending the rest of his days as an overly insistent advocate of a consciously bohemian hedonism. Free love, he argues, is an obligation—at least until his wife takes up with a sun-besotted hulk. The film's dialogue, like the effects in *Bjorn's Inferno*, is very much in the spirit of the action. With the exception of an especially sensitive scene in which the writer shuts up and listens to an elderly Spaniard, everyone's lines in the film sound like a bad imitation of avant-garde writing. But perhaps they should. For King, the problem of Ibiza was a familiar dilemma, the contradiction between utopian escapism (with its promise of unbounded self-expression) and the stolid bourgeois self-discipline of his background, which in the end enabled him to make something as demanding as a movie. There is a choice to be made between these two directions. In the last scene, the film's protagonist gathers up his family and leaves Ibiza.

King was on his way to doing the same.

The Actuality Dramas

King's decision to leave not only sunny Ibiza but also swinging London was the product of historical circumstances and what can only be called personal triumph. By the mid-1960s, Allan King Associates was thriving as the CBC's source for documentaries about Britain and Europe. Back in Canada, though, film was taking on an importance it had never previously known. At the National Film Board, Unit B had turned out one highly innovative documentary after another and was preparing to head in an entirely new direction: the technological wizardry to be seen at Expo 67. *Cinéma-vérité* documentaries like Pierre Perrault's *Pour la suite du monde* (1963) and the collectively made films of the Board's French unit (*Les Raquetteurs* [1958], *La Lutte* [1961], *À Saint Henri le cinq septembre* [1962] and many others) were cornerstones of the province's Quiet Revolution. And there was, at last, some consistency in feature film production. The tools of *cinéma-vérité* had made possible a New Wave of Canadian feature films: Claude Jutra's *À tout prendre* (1963), Don Owen's *Nobody Waved Good-bye* (1964), Gilles Carle's *La Vie heureuse de Léopold Z.* (1964), and Gilles Groulx's *Le Chat dans le sac* (1964). These and other features generated a growing demand for a federally subsidized Canadian film industry. In the heady days leading to the year-long celebration of the nation's Centennial, that appeared increasingly likely.

King was certainly contemplating his own position in this new Canadian film scene when he gave an interview to *Canadian Cinematography* in 1965:

> I would love to see the distinction between documentary and
> feature disappear and I think the notion of filmed drama is a

relatively pernicious one for it implies all the worst faults of television drama which tend to be that it is drama that doesn't effectively use the medium, and the medium is not creatively used. . . . But I would think that in this country one can think of doing longer, more ambitious films that incorporate a much more intensive kind of experience into film. I don't know how much one has to be concerned whether it's going into a theatre or television.[13]

At about this time, King made a proposal to the CBC producer Patrick Watson, for a documentary about children in a British school for the gifted. Watson countered that the school would have to be in Canada, that he would prefer it to be a school for emotionally disturbed children and that he had found just the place, right in Toronto. It was called Warrendale. King agreed to have a look.

Warrendale, finished in 1966 and released in 1967, transformed King from a journeyman Canadian filmmaker to an internationally recognized auteur. Part of the transformation had to do with the outcry that ensued when the CBC, after nearly a year of internal debate, decided not to broadcast the film. The reason given was that the Warrendale kids, when sufficiently agitated, used language then prohibited for broadcast—obscenities that would have been just barely admissible in theatrical films. King himself had wondered during the shoot how he would ever get the show on air and, from this perspective, the CBC's even considering the film might be seen as a positive sign. Moreover, the terms under which *Warrendale* was cancelled represented, in and of themselves, a rather humane, Canadian sort of repression. The CBC allowed King to distribute the film theatrically anywhere in the world and to sell it to networks outside of Canada.[14]

None of this influenced the outcry over *Warrendale* when the film opened theatrically in Canada and later in the

Warrendale

United States and Britain. In addition to eliciting a generalized protest against censorship, the film carried with it a considerable amount of more specific baggage. In 1966, while the film was being considered for broadcast, the CBC, its supporters and critics were embroiled in the turmoil over the cancellation of the network's outspoken news commentary program, *This Hour Has Seven Days*. *Warrendale*'s producer, Patrick Watson, was also *This Hour*'s executive producer and co-host (King had contributed a number of items from London). *This Hour*'s muckraking, its hosts' aggressive interviews and its merciless satire of official hypocrisy in prose and song led to very public exchanges between Watson and the CBC management—and ultimately to Watson's open defiance of management's orders to tone the program down. When *This Hour* was abruptly cancelled in the spring of 1966, Watson rallied a nationwide protest. He succeeded in getting a parliamentary inquiry into the cancellation and his own name was bandied about as the next president of the CBC (although *This Hour* would remain cancelled and it would be two decades before Watson won an executive position at the Corporation).

Internationally, the censorship battle over *Warrendale* was cited as yet one more battle between a generation stubbornly clinging to their power over the media and the younger generation wishing to displace them. With *cinéma-vérité*, documentary was changing from an instrument presenting voices of authority to a genre that sought to give a voice to the voiceless and show the unspeakable. Hence *Warrendale* took its place alongside Peter Watkins' docudrama *The War Game* (1966), which was banned by the BBC for making nuclear war seem rather unpleasant if not entirely un-British. The state of Massachusetts fought the release of Frederick Wiseman's film *Titicut Follies* (1967) when it shed a negative light on their decrepit bedlam for the criminally insane. King had already had a taste of the same sort of reaction in 1961, when he was reprimanded over *A Matter of Pride*. With *Warrendale*, King was accused of abusing the children simply because his film acknowledged their existence.

For people who viewed the film with any degree of open-mindedness, child abuse is exactly what did not happen. *Warrendale* became a *cause célèbre* not because its director was exploiting anyone but because he was, on the contrary, presenting its subject with great sensitivity. His success in

The film you are about to see is disturbing. It
ought to be - it's a completely spontaneous
record taken from five weeks filming in a treatment
home for emotionally disturbed children: Warrendale,
near Toronto, before its recent administrative
break-up.

Whatever the scientific explanation, and there are
many conflicting theories, the fact is that up to
10% of our children suffer from an emotional dis-
ability to cope with daily living ...

... some children withdraw from the "real" world,
others vent their hatred against the uncontrollable,
still others resort to futile cursing in an attempt
to allay their fears.

This film does not attempt to explain the medical
or social background of the children's illnesses;
nor is it a step-by-step illustration of a
particular mode of treatment.

Rather, it is an invitation to viewers to share
some of the experiences of children and staff, to
join them as they engage in the forceful communication of their feelings.

Staff members who appear in the film will be
present in the bearpit afterwards to discuss some
of the questions raised.

The model for treatment is
the ideal family in natural
surroundings. Hence the children
live together as a family unit
in the atmosphere of a normal
home. The staff's function
Physical non-verbal communication
base for communication
model of ideal family in nature
controls to suit community
therapeutic present
is to act as therapeutic parents
to provide security and controls;
most of all to react sensitively
to the individual needs of
each child.

You will notice the
emphasis placed on non-
verbal communication between
staff and children - through
feeling and holding in particular.
Adult speech patterns often have
no meaning to the disturbed child

creating both his own masterpiece and a milestone in the development of *cinéma-vérité* became evident almost immediately. Within a month of its cancelled broadcast date, *Warrendale* won the Prix d'art et essai at Cannes. It went on to share the British Academy Award with Antonioni's *Blow-Up* and the New York Critics' Award with Buñuel's *Belle de jour*. In 1968, Jean Renoir saw the film and wrote to Marshall Lewis, King's New York publicist, that *Warrendale* was the work of "a great artist."

Warrendale's observational, non-judgmental aesthetic was the product of everything King had developed in his first very busy decade as a filmmaker. In *Warrendale*, like *Skidrow* and *Rickshaw* (and unlike *Titicut Follies*), there is no case being made, no heroes or villains. In fact, the film's story, such as it is, has no outcome. King himself believed in the holding technique used with the Warrendale children, a therapy that allowed them to regress to a near primal state while keeping them physically secure as they acted out their deep anger and frustration. It is not an easy process to watch. The tension begins to rise from the first moments of the film, as the Warrendale staff challenge the children's actions and opinions. Why aren't they going easier on these volatile kids? We wait. Then as the film progresses, these challenges and the kids' reaction to them reshape what we are watching. Instead of cases to gawk at, the kids are seen as the complicated, charming and emotionally tortured humans they are. They become people precisely by defending their actions.

Our understanding of the Warrendale experience is tested in the film's climax, which, as captured by William Brayne, also serves as one of the defining moments of *cinéma-vérité*. Warrendale's cook, who has become a mother figure to many of the children, has suddenly and unexpectedly died. The children are gathered in the living room to be told the news. Some appear numbed by shock, others rage until they are restrained by the staff scrambling from one wounded child to the next. Some viewers see the children's behaviour as a setback in their treatment, while for others it is a justification of the holding therapy. As Wendy Michener suggested in *Maclean's*, the children's emotional reaction could be construed, for both them and us, as a moment of hope.

> The violence of the scene is unquestionably disturbing but it leads, as in tragedy, through terror and pity to a kind of release.

August 21, 1968

Mr. Marshall Lewis
6 Bank Street
New York, N.Y. 10014

Dear Marshall Lewis:

I am happy to know that you are a
participant in the adventure of "Warrendale".
Allan King is a great artist. His remarquable
work exposes one of the most suspenseful actions
I ever watched on a screen. You know how much
I love actors. When I think of this film the
best performances seem to me obsolete. How can
fiction, animated by professional players, compete
with this recording of real emotions. In
"Warrendale" you never feel the presence of the
camera or of the micrpphone. I am quite sure
that everything was recorded directly. I am
terribly conscious of dubbing. In "Warrendale"
I was under the impression of being hidden in a
corner of this children's hospital and of
actually witnessing the events registered on
the screen.

Oscar is happy to have news from you.
He sends you his best and my wife asks to be
remembered.

With my friendliest wishes,

Jean Renoir

To identify with the children in *Warrendale* is to identify with reality and this can lead us, like the best art, to deeper self-knowledge.[15]

Warrendale is also an autobiographical film. The residence in which the film was shot, like King's own childhood environment, is a home longing for stability. Caring parental figures, as many as any child could want, are in attendance. All are committed to providing emotional support. What is taught, again and again, by these parental figures is that actions have consequences, and that one will always have to account, in an emotional as well as practical sense, for one's choices. Perhaps because of the setting's relation to his own past, King established a unique rapport with both the Warrendale staff and the children. When one of the teenagers wondered whether she should let herself be filmed drinking from a baby bottle, King and the crew sat with her and drank from the same bottle. The result of this empathy is that King filmed Warrendale as one of the sanest places he had ever been, a true utopian community, an Ibiza in his own country.

Warrendale's successful theatrical release in Canada and abroad suggested to King that distributing his work in theatres was, at least for the moment, a realistic prospect. He took advantage of the situation with the second of what he was now calling actuality dramas. His proposal was to take his cameras into another, somewhat more familiar sanctuary, the home of a married couple:

> They will appear at first glance to be a typical married couple. But people are not generalities. They are individual, unique and special. The film will succeed in the degree to which it can draw out this uniqueness. At the same time, this acute observation of one individual situation, just because of its narrow and deep focus, will lead to a better understanding of all marriages.[16]

Billy and Antoinette Edwards, the two people King selected as the subjects of *A Married Couple* (1969), appeared to be ensconced in another sort of utopia. They were yet more Ibiza veterans who had, like the family in

Running Away Backwards, returned to Canada. There, thanks to Billy's lucrative job—and the union-scale wages they received for being in the film—they lived the lives of upper-tax-bracket citizens who were still not quite letting go of their bohemian past. As Ronald Blumer described them in his review of *A Married Couple*:

> The couple selected for this microscopic viewing is not a typical one. The husband is a witty ad copy writer and the wife is quite intelligent, or at least well educated. The objects with which their world is cluttered—the modern furniture, the Beatle records and the late model foreign car—are all typical of the well-off hip couple. The mental attitudes, their ideas of freedom, of women's rights versus male supremacy, are equally familiar scenery.[17]

What was less familiar about the Edwardses was the reason they were willing to participate in King's experiment. As King himself describes it:

> The adventure was certainly a great attraction; they were very nervy people, interested in exploration and new experience—as one might expect of a writer and a painter, both of them with the nerve to break out of the New York ad world to gamble on his ability to mature as a writer. But fundamental was their own recognition, which is a clear sub-text throughout the dialogue, that their marriage was in some difficulty and a marriage in conflict (this was their qualification for consideration as subjects for the film). The primary draw of taking part was the hope that they might discover the heart of the matter and change. That was why they insisted on the right to screen all the footage after it was shot, and did. Their goal was nobler than most gave them credit for. I thought their courage was outstanding.[18]

Even at a time when turning mercilessly bright lights on once hidden institutions was itself becoming something of an institution, *A Married Couple* was seen as especially audacious. The camera's purview extended into all corners of the Edwardses' life, from sleepy Antoinette welcoming the filmmakers into the bedroom as she awoke, through the couple's daily squabbles and finally back again to the bedroom, where the camera remained for at least the first stages of foreplay. This degree of intimacy elicited a predictable rejection from the guardians of public decorum (such as the Ontario Censor Board). What was slightly less predictable was a kind of denial by more sympathetic viewers: this couldn't really be happening. Was it actually possible to live real life in front of a camera crew? Roland Gelatt pondered the question in *Saturday Review*:

> No, it can't all be really real. But if we accept *A Married Couple* as occupying a midway point between *vérité* and intervention, the film seems far less problematical. Obviously, it could not have been made about any married couple. In Billy and Antoinette Edwards, King has found two remarkably verbal

A MARRIED COUPLE

Purpose

The object of the film is to explore /a real marriage *a crisis in* relationship between actual people. The form will be dramatic, the material actuality.

insert "X"

We will require the maximum candour which can be brought to bear by the married couple and the film makers, working together over a lengthy period of time, following the vicissitudes of the relationship as it is acted out in daily living. ¶ We will understand the couple's feelings as they are expressed in action, not through the filter of talk about them. That is to say, this is a film of ~~dramatic action~~ *experience*, not interview and comment.

The couple will have been married for perhaps five or ten years. They will probably have children. They are likely to be lower middle class. They ~~are city dwellers~~ ~~live in suburban Toronto~~, *stet* *live in suburban Toronto,* they could live anywhere in Western society. Place is not important.

They will appear at first glance to be a typical married couple. But we will see that they stand only for themselves. *But* People are not generalities. They are individual, unique, and special. This film, like any work of art, will succeed only in the degree to which it can draw out this uniqueness. At the same time, the acute observation of one individual situation, *just* because of its narrow and deep focus, *will* can lead to a better understanding of all marriages.

We will focus on a particular marriage crisis. It need not be cataclysmic; it may resolve happily or unhappily; it may not resolve at all. We will also strive to record those warm and happy moments which are the reward of an enduring relationship.

Above all —wherever it may lead — it is the honest expression of the dynamic of the relationship as expressed in acts which must be our concern and the concern of the couple in the film. Without this firm committment from the outset, the film would be impossible, a violation, and a fraud. With committment, some skill, some luck, and as much honesty as we can muster, a unique and pioneering experience is possible.

a married couple

the jones they're not

a new film by allan king

and outgoing protagonists. . . . Though they are not acting here in the conventional sense, they are most decidedly acting out—reiterating and replaying—the burdens and frustrations of their fractious relationship.[19]

For his part, King was and is less concerned with whether the Edwardses acted for the camera. As he would tell the *Globe and Mail* some years later:

It's always the case, in my experience, that the people you're filming use the camera, use the situation, for their own purposes. . . . It's not really a devious thing; it is simply wishing to be understood, or to share what they're trying to do—or trying to find out for themselves what it is they're doing."[20]

What were they doing? It was a question with a significant demographic aspect. Released in select theatres, *A Married Couple* became a kind of litmus test for "hip" couples, boomers and those suffering from boomer

A Married Couple

envy who were attempting to balance freedom with monogamy. Audiences were split, some empathizing with Billy, some with Antoinette, others with both or neither. From King's perspective these individual preferences were less important than the fact that audiences related strongly to the characters not just in terms of the film but of their own relationships. The film also taught him the extent to which audiences project their own vision upon a character.

> I learned more about "projection" and "projective identification" from audiences of the film than any other source. As an audience, we neglect the fact that what we experience in a theatre or on a tube are simply pictures and sounds of people drawn from a very small sample of a very small sample of their lives. Into these scraps of evidence we put in huge gobs (a lifetime's worth) of our own experience of assumptions based on our own personal experience and proceed to draw conclusions about these bits of emulsion on celluloid. Amazing the conclusions people reach and how much they reflect of themselves, so little of the objects external to them.[21]

27

Ultimately, the question posed in *A Married Couple* is not so much that of intimacy or manipulation as it is, yet again, the question of choice. If a secure environment permits free choice and choice inevitably has consequences, how secure will that environment remain? With this in mind, the conjugal tensions of *A Married Couple* segued into the communal dissolution King depicted in the third of his trilogy of actuality dramas, *Come On Children* (1973). He wanted to again make a film about adolescents, this time the ostensibly sane adolescents who had, in the sixties and early seventies, been acting out in highly noticeable ways. King's researcher, Phyllis Bassett, asked several hundred Canadian adolescents what they wanted. King then selected a cross-section, ten young people, and gave it to them, "it" being a place in the country, freedom from their parents and the resources to develop

Come On Children

themselves any way they saw fit. Once they had what they wanted, the kids'
choice was to do nothing. For long stretches of the film, the only thing
moving seems to be film running through the camera. Dishes and half-eaten
food pile up in the kitchen. Everyone must get stoned. When the self-
sedated subjects do speak, most are aggressively inarticulate. King himself
intervenes in an attempt at an interview and can elicit no more than a para-
noid brush-off. As John Hofsess wrote in a piece entitled "Allan King Ends
the Sixties":

> Ninety minutes pass. Not once do you hear a new or different
> idea. These kids aren't originators of anything. They wear their
> ratty hair, sad-sack clothes and antisocial attitudes like an ill-
> fitted costume rented for the duration of their adolescence.[22]

King himself is far more tolerant of the *Come On* children, arguing that
revelation and personal growth—much less profundity—were never part of
the deal they made with him. To judge them as failing by these criteria was
simply part of the habit of audience projection he had discovered with *A
Married Couple*. Anger at their hothouse hippie lives was nothing more
than another kind of acting out, this time by adults in their perpetual war
with youth. King has come to see the young people in the film another way:
simply as individuals undergoing a particular stage in their development,
people who for the most part survived the moment, and, perhaps despite
their intentions, let it change them for the better. "At any rate," King still

maintains, "I came to find the kids in the film charming, funny, full of delightful sass, and from them, finally, I learned an immeasurable lesson."[23]

Television Drama

Even before completing *Come On Children*, King realized that another sort of paradise was rapidly fading. The moment for taking over the theatres with counterculture films had come and gone. *A Married Couple*, although financed by the private network, CTV (which chose, in the end, not to broadcast the film) as well as private investors, did not recoup its costs. *Come On Children*, despite support from Famous Players, did even worse, never actually achieving its theatrical release.

As lab bills exceeded revenues at Allan King Associates, King returned to television drama. And here his timing could not have been better. By the early 1970s, thanks to the work of a few heroic individuals and Canada Council support bordering on adequate, English-Canadian theatre was enjoying a golden age. A generation of Canadian actors, playwrights and producers were creating minor miracles in Toronto's brand-new alternative theatres. For its part, the CBC was committed to the same kind of anthology drama programming that had, more than a decade before, given American television its golden age. Programs like *Anthology*, *Performance*, *To See Ourselves*, *Here to Stay* and *For the Record* were electronic stages that—with some determined prodding from young producers and filmmakers (including King)—mixed more established theatre and literary adaptations with the work of emerging Canadian talents.

Much of King's work in anthology drama was as the chronicler of English-Canadian theatre during this time of unprecedented success. He did so directly in a documentary, *Theatre in Canada* (1976), that leaves us with a sampler of a dozen or so actors in what can now be seen as classics of the period. King's film of Carol Bolt's Brechtian play, *Red Emma* (1976) is, in a more sophisticated way, very much like *The Field Day*, the record of a play shot by a crew on stage with the actors (and shot quickly—in this case in five days, while King was simultaneously shooting another production). In *Six War Years* (1975), King again combines documentary and drama, directing actors in the recreation of an oral history of Canadian experiences during the Second World War.

King's most important work in the 1970s and early 1980s was not simply to record the new English-Canadian theatre but to adapt it for television.

One Night Stand

In that process, he completed a long apprenticeship as a director of dramatic films. His first drama of the 1970s, *Mortimer Griffin, Shalinsky and How They Settled the Jewish Question* (1971), is an adaptation of a Mordecai Richler short story. It was only a small step beyond *Running Away Backwards*: the performances are uncertain and overblown, turning what might have been social commentary into farce, sometimes intentional and sometimes not. King, as usual, learned from his mistakes. In collaboration with the abundance of talent available to him, he grew quickly as a director of television drama. He directed two far more successful literary adaptations: *A Bird in the House* (1973), from a story by Margaret Laurence, and *Baptizing* (1975), a story by Alice Munro.

In 1978, King's adaptation of Carol Bolt's *One Night Stand* demonstrated how far he had come. The play is about a lonely, thirtyish single woman who brings home a much younger man to help her celebrate her birthday. Gradually we learn that this charming, Puckish figure is not the Ibiza refugee he seems; he is instead an unstable psychopath whose wild story about murdering a woman becomes increasingly believable. In adapting the play, King took the already claustrophobic stage set of the woman's studio apartment and squeezed it into the confines of the small tube. This box within a box is made smaller and smaller with each of the psychopath's revelations. As if filming *cinéma-vérité*, the camera stays close to the action, framing close-ups and tight two-shots of the principal characters. *One Night Stand* is, in this sense, the completion of King's many formal experiments with both staged realities and the use of documentary style to enhance a fictional realism.

King's television dramas also provided an opportunity to make what were, in everything but name, short feature films. The best of these was the

1977 production *Maria*, from an original script by Rick Salutin. Shot in black and white, the film is about a second-generation Italian Canadian who defies her traditional family and fearful co-workers by leading a union-organizing drive in a Toronto sweatshop. The story is told as humanized socialist realism. Typical of King's work, the film's characters are credited with motivations other than pure good and evil. The sweatshop owner may well believe that his employees are his extended family. Maria's wise father, a traditional patriarch played straight, is more saddened than angered by her rebellion. Maria herself is not free from the ethnic prejudices of her parents' generation. In the end, the union drive fails, leaving the bosses relieved, the union organizers despondent and only Maria with the knowledge that the fight was less political than personal, a matter of self-affirmation through choice.

Maria

While shooting *Maria*, King was also preparing to film his first theatrical feature, an adaptation of W. O. Mitchell's classic Canadian novel *Who Has Seen the Wind*. The film, like most Canadian features at the time, was made possible by the Canadian government's lucrative twin incentives. The Canadian Film Development Corporation, a federal agency formed in 1967, provided seed money for Canadian features, while the Capital Cost Allowance, an income tax credit originating in 1974, served as an even more attractive lure for investors.

Who Has Seen the Wind (1977) was one of the few critical and financial success stories of these early days of Canada's subsidized film industry. Despite the film's low budget, King succeeded in designing his own small world. At the core of that world was a familiar professional family. The script was adapted from Mitchell's novel by King's then wife, Patricia Watson, who had already worked with him on television dramas. Richard Leiterman was director of photography and the film was edited by Arla Saare, whom King had known from his first days at CBUT. King cast some familiar Canadian actors—Helen Shaver, Chapelle Jaffe and Gordon Pinsent—

along with a veteran Hollywood star, Jose Ferrer. After screen-testing some four thousand Saskatchewan boys, Patricia Watson found Brian Painchaud and Douglas Junor to play the children though whose eyes the story unfolds. King also recruited local filmmakers to work as interns on the shoot. The film's remaining star was Arcola, Saskatchewan, the place and its people, made over by King's crew into the Depression-era town of Mitchell's novel.

Who Has Seen the Wind

In King's career, *Who Has Seen the Wind* stands as the fictional equivalent of *Warrendale* in its realization of the sum of its director's talents and concerns. As Peter Harcourt points out elsewhere in this volume, the film's communal production is evident onscreen. *Who Has Seen the Wind* is also among King's most autobiographical productions, reproducing the anxieties he himself faced as a child learning the lessons of his close-knit community during the hard years of the 1930s. As Harcourt notes, King got the Depression right—capturing not just the era's iconography but its prevailing attitudes and speech patterns as well. Like so many of his documentaries, actuality dramas and chronicles of Canadian theatre, this too is a period piece, better for having been so deliberately intended as one.

The success of *Who Has Seen the Wind* led to a second, much more generously budgeted feature, *Silence of the North* (1981). Produced by Universal Films, it was set in the 1920s and starred Ellen Burstyn as a woman trying to survive both the Alberta wilderness and her husband's romantic delusions about it. The film has some effective scenes and benefits from Richard Leiterman's landscape photography. For King, though, *Silence of the North* was a Hollywood production in the most negative possible way, ending in a destructive, losing battle for creative control. At one point, he considered taking his name off the project. Instead, taking what he now sees as bad advice, King resigned himself to the fact that what had begun with Patricia Knop's strong script about the awakening to self-knowledge of a unique woman would end as nondescript entertainment made by a very unhappy committee.

Who's in Charge?

What happened in the wake of *Silence of the North* is typical of King's life-long habit of thinking through the lessons of a disaster. Losing control of his own film led him to reflect on questions that had, he realized, haunted all his films: the nature of work, choice and responsibility. He read widely and made inquiries of people in a number of fields. The psychoanalyst Sheldon Heath referred him to the Tavistock Institute, a British-based research centre with a mandate to study the practical applications of social science concepts. King attended Tavistock's annual ten-day conference on authority, leadership and organization, and while there discussed with one of the institute's co-directors the possibility of arranging and filming his own conference, using the Tavistock approach to address unemployment.

Who's in Charge?, King's first CBC documentary since *Warrendale*, created a public furor of similar intensity. As was the case with *Warrendale*, this upset should not have been a surprise. King sought to explore the nature of work by concentrating on people who had been deprived of it. As he had already learned in *A Matter of Pride*, the topic of unemployment was highly loaded both emotionally and politically. This was especially true in the deep recession of the early 1980s. When King set about selecting a representative sample of the unemployed, he had a wide pool from which to draw. Blue-collar workers, white-collar workers, union and non-union, men, women and industrial and resource-sector workers, people from every region of Canada—all had suffered.

It might have been assumed that King would simply document these individuals' despair, as he had done in *A Matter of Pride*. In fact, what he planned had less to do with documentary, even his own practice of it, than with the use of a uniquely television-based format, the electronic town-hall meeting. King contracted thirty unemployed workers to participate in a four-day conference headed by Gordon Lawrence of the Tavistock Institute. Brochures and telephone calls to the participants emphasized that the conference would be about sharing their stories of unemployment or, for that matter, any other experiences that the group identified as pertinent. King recruited the CBC's best drama crew to record the event, limiting them to filming only within the room and during the hours in which the working sessions of the conference were held. The cameras were also denied access to the carpeted area on which the participants' chairs were arranged. This was to be their space.

When the conference opened and the red lights lit up on the video cameras, Lawrence, the other facilitators and the thirty unemployed Canadians sat in silence, each waiting for the other to speak. It was an awkward moment and the moments that followed were more awkward still. Conference participants began speaking on their own, only to become increasingly impatient with the lack of response from the group of experts facing them. Direct questions went unanswered. The sparse interventions by the facilitators offered no concrete answers. Most were simply observations on the evolving group dynamics. From the facilitators' perspective, the lack of response served a logical if unannounced purpose: not directly answering until all the questions that the group had to ask had been asked. This was seen as a way to ensure that all possible avenues had been opened before any were explored. But for the participants and many of the documentary's

Who's in Charge?

viewers, the silence looked like arrogance. As in *Warrendale*, the novelty of an unconventional approach to human interaction produced a growing tension. Who is going to explode? When? How? The tension was further increased when, at the precise moment each session was scheduled to end, no matter who was speaking or what they were saying, the facilitators silently rose and walked out of the room. This too had a rationale in the Tavistock method: starting and ending work exactly on time—even without advising participants of the importance that would be attached to doing so—was seen by Lawrence and the other facilitators as a necessary appreciation of the finiteness of time and its value.

By the end of the conference, there are explosions: a chair is thrown at the facilitators and one participant storms out. As King would later argue, these and other highly uncomfortable moments were not the point of either the conference or the documentary he made of it. Instead, the entire Tavistock method was designed to get past facile expressions of pain and clichés of victimhood. Its purpose was to allow the participants to take charge of their own responses to their unemployment and, either individually or collectively, to work through those responses toward a positive outcome. This was never conceived as an easy or polite process. Lawrence himself tells the participants toward the end of the program: "I am here to help you to get your authority, whether you like it or not!"

King's purpose in making the television documentary was to allow a wider audience to share, to whatever extent possible, both this method and its outcome. In some ways, his creation of empathy worked all too well. Broadcast in September 1983, *Who's in Charge?* was met with more shock and anger than anything King had ever made. Even before the broadcast, a small group of the participants sought an injunction from the Ontario Supreme Court to prevent the work from being aired. This time, the CBC stood behind King and endured considerable abuse not only from the litigants but also from audiences and critics. This was not a documentary about public tears or foul-mouthed teenagers. King was accused of inflicting on Canada the spectacle of already vulnerable people being treated with no visible sympathy by rather comfortable-looking professionals. At the Grierson Film Seminar, an annual symposium of documentary filmmakers and students of the genre, an argument over King's treatment of the unemployed erupted into a fistfight. There was, as other critics pointed out, a broader political context. This was a moment when Canada's relatively benevolent social safety net was being challenged by the rise of Thatcherism and Reaganomics (and shortly thereafter by the election of Brian Mulroney as Canada's own neo-conservative prime minister). The left argued that this was not the moment to examine unemployment in terms of individual responsibility. Michael Dorland wrote in *Cinema Canada* that it was a time for taking sides:

> . . . it is perhaps on the question of novelty that the import of *Who's in Charge?* becomes clear. In part, the novelty was the program's emotionalism: in the anger and frustration of the unemployed participants; in their tears and confessions of suicidal thoughts; in their depiction, finally, of contemporary society's dirty little secret; namely that human social experience is anguishing because it consists of the infliction of pain by the powerful against the powerless.
>
> But to identify the infliction of the pain experienced by a small social group for the entertainment of a larger social group is to understand it as sadism. And it was the sadism of the program that constituted the real novelty of *Who's in Charge?*, Allan King's contribution to the sinister television documentary of the future.[24]

King defended the film in an exchange of articles in *Cinema Canada*. *Who's in Charge?*, he asserted, was exactly what he intended it to be, a defiance of the prevailing cult of the victim. Unemployment and the devastation it wrought would not be presented as "the disease of the week" or that night's social crisis item on the six o'clock news. If King pursued the issue on a personal, even psychoanalytical level, it was because he believed that it was on that level that it might be more profitably addressed. In his defence of the program, King marshalled his readings on psychology and small group dynamics to propose what amounted to a regime of personal therapy. Avoidance could be avoided. The all-powerful father figure could be rejected. The result, he suggested, would be real, lasting change—not only

Participants from *Who's in Charge?*

among the unemployed but also in the wider audience who had viewed the program and through this vast audience, society itself.

> *Who's in Charge?* explores the experience of being unemployed; painful feelings of helplessness, panic, rage and depression. What we discovered was that when we allow ourselves to "experience the experience" (to use the words of Austin Lee) we are able to mobilize our strength, anger and even humour; we become articulate, full of fight and begin to take charge of our own lives again.
>
> What was startling was the need for some of the audience to see the unemployed as helpless victims, inarticulate and pathetic, confirming Gordon Lawrence's notion that society needs victims: for example, the unemployed, to carry our shitty feelings of helplessness and deprivation. . . . The notion also explains in part (obviously there is much more) the perseverance of unemployment in the richest, most skillful society mankind has ever known.
>
> *Who's in Charge?* also exemplified Wilfrid Bion's description of the way large groups (club, tribe, society, the state, take your pick) unconsciously avoid the pursuit of their avowed task; in the pursuit of the omnipotent leader who will do our work for us; the discovery of a magic text which will save us the trouble of thinking for ourselves; the flight into irrelevant activity; the search for a scapegoat; and, finally, identification with the group as a mystical entity which will save us from harm (Pierre Turquet's notion).[25]

As may be seen in the interview with him elsewhere in this volume, King maintains his position to this day. But in 1983, the stress of defending *Who's in Charge?*—and the financial drain it had brought to his company—once again turned him away from documentary filmmaking and back to the dramatic film.

Back in Charge

Since the mid-1980s, most of King's film work has been as a director of episodes of American television series shot in Canada. The best that may be said of these is that the money is good and making American television in Canada is, to paraphrase Peter Ustinov's crack about Toronto, like Burbank run by the Swiss. Scripts and talent arrive pre-negotiated, Canadian crews have become ferociously competent and if there are any problems they land on the desk of an equally ferocious "show runner." King's role as director has been to carefully plan the shoots and establish a productive working relationship with the cast and crew. Of the many television episodes he has directed, some of the most satisfying have been those for *Alfred Hitchcock Presents* and for the American-Canadian series *The Road to Avonlea*. The latter pits the sunny paradise of Edwardian Prince Edward Island against the characters' deeply felt emotional trials. King won Best Director at the 1993 Gemini Awards for one episode and Christopher Lloyd, his lead actor in another episode, won an Emmy for it in 1992. These awards as well as his long list of television episode credits are some indication that King's working methods are widely appreciated.

Termini Station

King has also made one more feature. *Termini Station* (1989) stars Colleen Dewhurst and Megan Follows as an alcoholic mother and her self-loathing daughter trapped in dead-end lives. The film is set in Kirkland Lake, an Ontario mining town depicted as a kind of scar in the bush around it. It is within this setting that the script—written by his wife, Colleen Murphy—returns to King's recurrent themes. The film's plot centres on the trauma and despair that result from the clash of the girl's two fathers. One is the dashing outsider who once had an affair with her mother but deserted her; he turns out to be the girl's biological parent. The other is the once loving man who believed he was her father and who, upon learning of his wife's betrayal, disowns and tries to kill his daughter, before taking his own life.

Redemption comes with the painful efforts of these two damaged women to face their various truths and, at last, to leave both their past and the town behind.

Whatever pleasures he may have enjoyed from his television work and *Termini Station*, Allan King continued to think about documentary. He

returned to the genre in 1998 with *The Dragon's Egg: Making Peace on the Wreckage of the Twentieth Century*. That project, like *Who's in Charge?* was the product of another personal inquiry. This time, the subject was ethnic prejudice. And the psychoanalyst King's research led him, via Sheldon Heath, to a group of experts, Vamık Volkan and his Center for the Study of Mind and Human Interaction at the University of Virginia. Volkan took King to Estonia, where his group had been hired to help resolve the tensions between Estonians and the ethnic Russians who had been left behind after the collapse of the Soviet Union. The title of the film itself summarizes that conflict. It is the phrase used by Estonians to describe the Russians Stalin had settled among them and whom they feared as a demographic time bomb. Also lingering over this particular society is an invisible history of conflict, a history that would be made somewhat less invisible by King's insertion of historical footage and interviews with old people who remember Stalin's and Hitler's atrocities.

The Dragon's Egg was commissioned not by the CBC but by the provincial public broadcaster, TV Ontario. It is a small, eye-level film shot in video; what plot there is focuses on a group of Russians and Estonians in a poor region of the country, who are given $50,000 by Volkan's Center on the condition that they work together to define and complete a useful project. The project they choose is the renovation of a deserted building to use as a community centre. If anything, the experiment goes *too* well— at least for the film's purposes. The group, led by a particularly engaging half-Estonian, half-Russian woman, holds meetings and makes its way over a few bureaucratic hurdles. There is more than enough time to talk and even

The Dragon's Egg

to party. But in the present-day Estonia we actually find in *The Dragon's Egg*, no one seems to have any problem with anyone else's politics or ethnicity. There is a minor conflict with a unemployed member of the organizing committee who finds it hard to have to accept work from his fellow committee members. His concerns are addressed. Whatever other small problems arise are easily subsumed in the group's chief worry about how they will provide for their children's future in the desolate post-Communist landscape. It is this happy surprise of ethnic harmony, this failure of even the film's own preconceptions, that is the true payoff for King's patient observation.

The Dragon's Egg

The film also leaves us with some personal, close-up, social and political insights. At one moment in the film some of the Russians are taking a break, and having downed a few cognacs are somewhat distracted from both their project and the film being made about it. One man remarks, "We all hoped to see Communism one day." Another replies instantly: "Then we realized we were already living in Communism." It is an off-hand observation but its larger meaning chimes like a cracked bell. For these are all people who have fallen out of one of history's grand narratives, the promise of a workers' paradise. Their poor corner of rural Estonia, standing strangely naked without its ideological garb, offers nothing but sporadic work and an uncertain future. In asking us to contemplate the Russians and Estonians, King is also inviting us to consider how far we too have fallen from grand narratives and their much-postponed happy endings—and suggests that in the end, this may not be such a bad thing.

Conclusion?

Drawing conclusions about the career of a living artist is a necessarily tentative undertaking. Allan King is far from finished with his life's work. As of this writing, he is preparing to shoot a documentary on the subject of death and dying. There is another documentary in the research and planning stage. King has written about his films in papers delivered at academic conferences and he is also writing about himself, finding time to revisit the long-neglected project of his memoirs. Another new venture is his teaching master classes to aspiring documentary filmmakers. And, quite rightly, he is enjoying the various tributes that come to a president emeritus of the Directors' Guild of Canada and an elder statesman of his nation's cinema.

In the first forty-six years of King's films, there has been nothing to match the spike of audience and critical response he received at the time of the "actuality dramas": *Warrendale*, *A Married Couple* and, to a lesser extent, *Come On Children*. These were works that shaped the first generation of *cinéma-vérité* and became part of the subgenre's textbook definition.

This is literally true in Alan Rosenthal's 1971 book, *The New Documentary in Action: A Casebook in Film Making*, where the discussion of *A Married Couple* consumes some forty-three pages of printed text. The status of King's films as classics of the genre is even more apparent when they are compared with the work of *cinéma-vérité*'s other auteurs. What was originally touted as an entirely transparent cinematic window had by the late 1960s fragmented into a number of perspectives and styles, reflecting the disparate interests of its practitioners. Jean Rouch and Pierre Perrault had created an observational, anthropological school of *cinéma-vérité*. The Americans had both their real-life action stories and, thanks to the success of Pennebaker's *Don't Look Back* (1967), the beginnings of a very lucrative use of *cinéma-vérité* to record musical performance; Frederick Wiseman had embarked on his annual critiques of American institutions; and radical filmmakers like Emile de Antonio, Howard Alk, Jean-Luc Godard's Dziga Vertov group and in Canada, the entire Challenge for Change program at the National Film Board, were using their documentary cameras as weapons in political struggle.

King—too subjective to be anthropological, not interested in documenting rock concerts, tolerant of institutions and alienated from Marxist politics—defined *cinéma-vérité* from yet another perspective. At one level his approach is simply an eclectic defiance of the original divisions within *cinéma-vérité*. King could be either a fly on the wall or an acknowledged onscreen participant. He could shape a film around a narrative element like the death of the cook in *Warrendale*, which comes at the end of the film even though, in fact, it took place toward the beginning of the shoot, or, as in *Come On Children*, King could live with a loose story, a sampling of reality. His creation of the situations in which he films adds another dimension to what *cinéma-vérité* can be. In *Come On Children* and later in *Who's in Charge?* King creates, and tells us he is creating, both the location and the ground rules for the film's action. He is not finding the action so much as provoking and isolating it—for a purpose. Within the carefully constructed crucibles of the hippie farm and the conference room respectively, people protected from the larger realities that brought them to the location are forced to face both the camera and themselves. As a result, King elicits from them a kind of psychology *vérité*, a wide range of reactions to a narrow range of circumstances.

The unique intent of King's project within *cinéma-vérité* goes some distance toward justifying his awkward and now discarded term, "actuality drama." These films are dramatic in the sense that their stories are contained within the Aristotelian unities of time, place and action. They are also dramatic in using this kind of containment to focus our attention on the relatively restricted choices by which these people can define themselves in this situation. They are dramatic in a third sense, in keeping with the convergence of fiction and non-fiction that many artists experimented with at the time they were released. The sixties had seen Truman Capote's positing of the idea of a nonfiction novel, Andy Warhol elevating pop culture icons into high art and even top-forty music turning its attention to documenting social realities. King's documentary treatment of the real world reached its maturity at exactly a moment when the borders between the important and quotidian were at their most vulnerable.[26]

King's historical timing was also fortunate—and formative—in that his career coincided with the rise of television. While many filmmakers, especially in Canada, have come to depend on television for both their living and the distribution mechanism for their films, few have spent their careers so completely within it as Allan King. All his documentaries other than *Come On Children* were made for television, as were all his fictional films other than the three features (two of which could not have been financed without television windows). Television gave King an instant response to his work and provided an avenue for his work to reach a large audience. Within television, he worked almost exclusively for the CBC until the late 1970s. Despite a sporadically stormy relationship with the public broadcaster and a deeper sense of disappointment at many of its lost opportunities and failures of vision, the net result of working within this milieu is a sense of purpose to King's work in both documentary and drama. Each of these films is about *something*. That something may be a Canadian or foreign social issue, it may be the evocation of a sensibility or a milieu (the bohemian films), it may explore some aspect of literary or theatrical culture, or, as in *Who's in Charge?* it may be a challenge to people's preconceptions of what constitutes an issue and how that issue may be presented. The common denominator in this work is a certain curb on self-indulgence in favour of work aimed at provoking a national dialogue.

The CBC also served to anchor King within Canada. Given his interest in intense psychological truth, it may seem odd that King would choose to work in an English-Canadian culture not known for its appreciation of displays of emotion, but he had experienced that emotional repression and availed himself of the opportunity to attack it from within the belly of the beast. The result of his work, after so many years, is a hard-won compromise. King's Canada lies somewhere between the beautiful but stifling mountain-bound paradise of his childhood and the unsustainable freedom of a bohemian life in distant and imagined cultures. It is a middle way between living a quiet domestic life and escaping to follow your dream, between working for the insurance company and living like a poet, between fantasizing revolution and succumbing to despair, as we find in *Who's in Charge?* Canada is like Warrendale, the Tavistock Institute, or the Center for the Study of Mind and Human Interaction; for that matter it is like the CBC, a challenging, often frustrating, though, when all is said and done, a nurturing institution, a home. Canada is King's own ultimate choice as a citizen and as an artist, though in the course of his long career he has lived in other places, many of which are more conducive to the filmmaker's art. But despite his deep roots in his native country, in his best work he speaks to his contemporaries anywhere in the world. Canadian audiences gave him his voice, a voice of complex and universal humanity.

1. Sadoul was paying homage to the early Soviet filmmaker Dziga Vertov, whose films and numerous polemics had insisted on taking the camera to the streets and keeping it there. Vertov's *Kinopravda* (1922–1925)—the term Sadoul translated into *cinéma-vérité*—was a newsreel series that looked nothing like *Chronique d'un été*. Even in his more mature works, *The Man with the Movie Camera* (1929) and *Enthusiasm* (1930), Vertov was equally interested in a highly formal use of film editing, not to mention the necessary inclusion of a heavy-handed Party line.

2. As we shall see, their task might have been simplified if they had recognized a third, more inclusive, definition of what they were doing, the term "Candid Eye" as used by the filmmakers at the National Film Board's Unit B since 1957. The Canadians made films that incorporated both styles. They also exported the practice, the best of their francophone and anglophone filmmakers collaborating with the French and Americans.

3. Vertov saw this coming. "If a fake apple and a real apple are filmed so that one cannot be distinguished from the other on the screen," he wrote in one of his manifestos, "this is not ability but incompetence—the inability to photograph. The real apple must be filmed in such a way that no counterfeit can be possible."

4. Doug Saunders, "Vérité Vision: He Likes to Listen," *Globe and Mail* (31 March 1999), C2.

5. "Memories of *Maria*" (manuscript), 1.

6. "Escape Artist," in *An Allan King Retrospective* (Montreal: La Cinémathèque canadienne, 1966), unpaginated.

7. Ibid., unpaginated.

8. "Almost a Canadian Classic," in *An Allan King Retrospective*, unpaginated.

9. "The White Island: Coming of Age in Ibiza," *Montage* (Spring 2001): 37.

10. "Notes on My Craft," in *An Allan King Retrospective*, unpaginated.

11. Author's correspondence with Allan King, 30 May 2002.

12. The same experiment was also undertaken by the New York avant-garde filmmakers Jonas and Adolphus Mekas, who filmed the entire play and released their work in 1964. The comparison with King's version is instructive, as the Mekas brothers shot the play largely in long shot and with

45

considerably less editing of their takes. King was unaware of the Mekas version and has not as of this writing seen it.

13. "Conversations on Film with Allan King," *Canadian Cinematography* 4, no. 4 (May–June, 1965): 13.

14. In 1995, the CBC sold King the Canadian television rights as well.

15. "The Brilliant Canadian Film You Can't See," *Maclean's* 80, no. 7 (July 1967): 6.

16. Allan King, "A Married Couple," typewritten proposal, unpaginated.

17. "A Married Couple," *Take One* 2, no. 4 (March–April 1969): 22.

18. Feldman-King correspondence, 30 May 2002.

19. "Marriage without a Script," *Saturday Review* (24 January 1970): 47.

20. Saunders, C2.

21. Feldman-King correspondence, 30 May 2002.

22. "Allan King Ends the Sixties, Everybody Waved Goodbye," *Maclean's* 84, no. 3 (March 1972): 86.

23. Feldman-King correspondence, 30 May 2002.

24. "Pawns of Experience," *Cinema Canada*, no. 102 (December 1983): 24.

25. "*Pourquoi?* Round Two," *Cinema Canada* no. 159 (January 1989): 5.

26. It might also be worth noting that King's own sensibility was the product of the 1930s, an era characterized by an elevated appreciation of documentary reality. Another such time is the present, when reality and fiction are in a sense amalgamated as they are both widely discussed—at least in academic circles—as being nothing more than social constructs.

Allan King

Apprenticeship

My first film, *Skidrow*, was one of the earliest examples of what would later be called the West Coast School of filmmaking. It was followed by a number of other "West Coast" films—first, documentaries and then, later, dramatic films. Each had a distinctive flavour and feel; each reflected a strong personality and temperament. In reality, though, our "school" came about through a concurrence of events, most of which had to do with pure happenstance.

For us, in Vancouver, the biggest surprise of these films was perhaps that they happened at all. Growing up in the 1930s and 1940s, we never imagined that we would be making films in our own home town. Until the CBC opened its television station, CBUT, in 1954, most of us thought of filmmaking as taking place only in unapproachably glamorous Hollywood or at the NFB in Montreal—a very small studio, and already full up. Of my UBC contemporaries, only Daryl Duke actually got a job in film, at the National Film Board of Canada. But he had taken creative writing with Earle Birney, the distinguished Canadian poet, and thought of himself as a poet as well. George Robertson, another of Birney's students, went on to take creative writing at Iowa University, got a job at the Board and then moved back to Vancouver as a radio producer.

My school chum (and later, brother-in-law) Rolph Blakstad *was* a certified artist. He won an Emily Carr scholarship to paint—an almost unimaginable career in Canada. He later put me straight on the matter of art. He was my first cinematographer when I became an independent producer, and he explained that *he* was the artist and I, as the producer, was the businessman—and that by being clear about this we would flourish. In any case, I never thought of myself as a creative person at all (and still don't).

But Rolph was right in that I did have a certain knack for running things. And one of those things was the Vancouver Film Society. In 1946, a mad and passionate cinephile, Vernon van Sickle, had revived the Vancouver Film Society; his magnificently ambitious (foolhardy, really) program of 35mm foreign features—Jean Renoir, Marcel Carné, Jean Vigo and the like at the Paradise Theatre once a month for the winter season, and a marvellous string of 16mm classics, including *Greed*, *Potemkin*, *Storm Over Asia* and many more—was the beginning of my education in film. My friend Stan Fox discovered the program, and insisted that I, too, get tickets, not just to the sound films but also for the silents.

With the near-collapse of the society in 1947 (because of its overly ambitious first year) and its rescue by Dorothy Burritt, a remarkable heroine of film culture in Canada, Stan and I took over as projectionists, music scorers and disc-spinners. In 1948, when Dorothy left Vancouver for Toronto, she encouraged Stan and me to rise from the ranks of worker/projectionists and join the film society's board. With brilliant insight, Stan also assumed the role of program director and assigned me that of secretary-treasurer. I soon discovered that if you don't call meetings (the secretary's job) you don't have to keep minutes and you can do as you like. I learned the value and virtues of bookkeeping much later, at a painful cost. But in truth, our board was remarkably indulgent, giving us their support and our heads; in return Stan and I ran the society well. By the 1950–51 season we had the use of a fine new theatre at the Vancouver General Hospital. We were packing in audiences and building a useful surplus.

Stan and I soon made the remarkable discovery that as film society programmers we could get films to "preview" for possible booking. We could not afford to book and preview 35mm films—the cost of screening facilities

Allan King at nineteen (1949)

was prohibitive. But I got a cast-off 16mm sound projector from the NFB and we screened, over a few years, virtually the entire catalogue of the Museum of Modern Art. It was a priceless education in film, virtually unattainable anywhere at the time and hard to come by even today. In fact, what we grew up to think of as classics—the German expressionist and Russian silent films, the French and Italian pre- and post-war classics—are still not readily accessible.

The Vancouver Film Society also inspired Stan to begin making films, mobilizing the rest of our group as actors and crew. He bought and modi- fied an RCAF gun-camera to run at sixteen frames a second—silent-film speed. He inherited an extraordinary processor and printer devised and built by Oscar Burritt, Dorothy's husband, who later became the first tech wizard at the CBC when it went into television. The processor was simply an oil barrel cut in half lengthwise; one of the halves was used as a tub for developing fluid. Film was wrapped around a rig made of two wooden bar- rel ends stuck at either end of a steel rod, with stainless steel bits soldered onto stainless steel wires running between them. We could wrap a hundred feet of 16mm film around the wires in the dark and process film—original or prints. Oscar's remarkably original and ingenious printer was simply a 16mm sprocketed synchronizer, with a rheostat-controlled viewing light that shone on the film as it was wound through. The faster one wound the film through the synchronizer, the brighter the light and greater the exposure; the slower one wound it, the dimmer the light. Exposure was thus automatically compensated, and once an exposure had been established by testing it was maintained. We processed hundred-foot samples of *The Days of Wrath*, *Potemkin* and other silent classics and hung them up to dry in Stan's basement.

Stan also managed to scrounge short ends of reversal film printing stock from the local film lab for nothing. The stock was so slow that only a sunny beach at high noon would provide a bright enough light for adequate exposure. So that was where we made our first film, *Glub*. It was actually Stan, Rolph and Norman Newton's film. I was just the stagehand and learned a lesson that lasted me a lifetime: I am lousy at taking or giving cues. I suffer from stage fright, and it has taken me half my career not to overcome but to manage it. The film was a parody of the surrealist films of Maya Deren and Boris Kaufman. It won an honourable mention at the Canadian Film Awards in 1950 and was quite funny.

For me, though, the making of the film had nothing to do with the beginning of a career. In fact, I had no idea what I was going to do for a living. As university came to an end, I took my philosophy professor's advice, and my new wife, Phyllis, and I took off for the "Grand Tour" of Europe. Actually, I left before finishing UBC. But I did finish my education, visiting virtually every one-, two- and three-star *objet d'art* in every gallery, building and museum lying south of a line from Bruges to Vienna and down to Paestum in the boot of Italy. Phyllis and I stayed on another summer, did Greece, then headed north through Yugoslavia and Germany into Scandinavia.

Early June of 1954 found us in Copenhagen, where I picked up a telegram from Stan Fox. He said that he'd just got a job as an assistant editor at the CBC. They were opening up a television station in Vancouver and every damn fool in town was getting a job there. If I hurried back, even I might get one. You didn't have to know anything!

Phyllis and I hitchhiked back to London as fast as we could and got student tickets on a LOT Airlines DC4 for New York. We grabbed a Greyhound for an overnight ride to Toronto and arrived with about two dimes left in our pockets. The first went for a call to Norman Campbell and his wife, Elaine, Phyllis's sister. Nobody home. They'd gone to Vancouver on holiday. The second dime got us to John Reeves, who had got work as a radio producer in Toronto. He was tied up preparing *Harmony Harbour* for broadcast that night. So he invited us to meet him at the studios at 11 p.m. (where we met the then unknown and very young Glenn Gould, who dropped in nightly to practise at the end of the broadcast day). John then took us home, put us up for the night and loaned us enough money for the four-day drive to Vancouver. In those days General Motors had a splendid scheme whereby you could drive a Chevy from their factory in Oshawa to a car lot in Vancouver for the price of gas. They even paid for the oil change.

We drove across the continent in three days, virtually non-stop—I knew I had to get there by Saturday night so I'd have Sunday to relearn how to thread a projector, splice and rewind film and qualify as an assistant editor. We made it. I turned up at Stan's on Sunday to learn my trade in time for my appointment Monday morning at ten, which had been arranged from London, with the program director, Marce Munro.

"Sorry, Mr. Munro just left for Toronto. He'll be back on Thursday."

Welcome to the world of television. But I did get a job: two weeks' work as an assistant film editor for the British Empire Games, which was the trial by fire for the launch of CBUT. Mobile trucks, our own and others sent out from Toronto, covered the events at Empire Stadium and the university. Signals were fed to the studio for kinescope recording—pointing a 16mm camera at the screen and shooting it. There was film coverage as well, but kinescopes were the heart of the matter. The rest of the world ran on 35mm gauge film. But the CBC, on the advice of Oscar Burritt, chose 16mm as a matter of economy. Later, Oscar's choice would have a dramatic and largely unnoticed impact on the development of documentary filmmaking and particularly *cinéma-vérité*. At the time, though, the result was less focus, less grading of tones from black through grey to white, and of course bigger grain.

I have two enduring memories from the two-week run of those Games and my first paying job in film. One was the sound of Arla Saare pounding down the corridor from the editing room to the telecine room, seconds before the seven o'clock airtime for the nightly news of the Games, the film still damp from the processor, the glue on the splices just dry. We would throw the reel up on the telecine projector and thread it, then push the buttons to send the pictures out over the Vancouver lower mainland. Arla was our goddess—a formidable Finn, frighteningly severe, passionately devoted to film, work, good Scotch and poker. She was also intensely shy, with a tendency to stutter under stress, hence not awfully talkative, but a woman with a wonderful sense of humour. The corners of her eyes had an utterly captivating crinkle as she got to the heart of a good story. We were in awe of her. She had worked at the Film Board in the days of Grierson—this was a woman to be attended to. And we did attend: her discipline and her devotion to the art and practice of filmmaking provided a model that has stood me in good stead ever since.

The second vivid memory was a life lesson in my technical aptitude—or lack thereof. While the rest of the studio was wrapped up in the daily rush of the Games, I came for the evening and night shift; I helped Homer Powell put kinescope recordings on 1,200-foot reels, stow them in cans, label them and send them out for delivery to the world. Homer was a remarkably wise, reflective and gentle film editor from Hollywood. He was in Vancouver in 1954 thanks to the red scare, which chased some of America's best and brightest north of the border. I was doubly in awe of Homer because he had actually worked in Hollywood, where filmmaking was a way of life, and because his reticence and wry humour were the opposite of the Hollywood stereotype. He eventually returned south, ending up in New York as supervising editor for the fabulously funny *Barney Miller* television show.

One lesson Homer gave me in how to manage catastrophe has been invaluable. It came during the single greatest moment of the games: the Bannister-Landy miracle mile. Roger Bannister, a Brit, had broken the unbreakable barrier of the four-minute mile. Shortly after that John Landy, an Aussie, had beaten his time. The two were to be matched at the Games. The world—or at least the British Commonwealth and Empire—was agog.

The start of the race was wrung with suspense—not just who would win, but how Landy's blistered heel would affect the outcome—and one image branded its climax: Landy, leading into and down the home stretch, looking over his shoulder then—what?—stumbling?—losing stride, focus, nerve? Whatever it was, Bannister came flying by and won.

Great Britain and all of Australia were waiting to see it. The kinescopes came in fresh from the lab. V-bombers were revved up at the airport (or at least in my mind they were). Homer looked after the Brits; I had the Aussie package. I pulled out the first reel of film, slapped it onto split reels, cinched them up, thrust the reel onto the rewind, stuck the head of the film to the take-up reel and began to crank as fast as I could go. Just as I passed the halfway mark, the growing girth of the take-up began rapidly to exceed that of the unwinding side, and its leverage multiplied dramatically. The feeder reel whizzed around at tremendously increasing speed, flew off the rewind and spun yards and yards of film high in the air and across the room. And snapped! In many places! I was crushed.

To me that moment marked a significant dividing line; behind it lay the Depression and the years before the second World War; after it, a new world. According to all the stories I had been told as a kid growing up before the war, I should have been fired on the spot. But it was 1954, and despite my gift for absentmindedness and less than stellar technical skills, I did not get canned. Instead I stayed with the job until it and the Games came to an end. Then, in August and September 1954, I went back to driving a taxi, exactly what I had been doing before leaving on my Grand Tour.

I never drifted very far from CBUT, which was quickly developing into Vancouver's creative centre. The studio was new and so was the medium. No one had yet learned to manage and diminish differences. So the people who worked there were allowed and even encouraged to speak in their own voices. On the West Coast, perhaps because air travel was still relatively expensive and infrequent, the rest of the world seemed very far away. No one was intimidated by New York or Europe. Distance protected us from the Second City syndrome, which the theatre critic Clive Barnes identified in Toronto: a parallel of the Second Critic syndrome, whereby the second critic on a paper feels the play he or she has to review must be inferior, because if it were not, the first critic would have been assigned. We weren't close enough to any original source to feel like anyone's second pick.

And so, after its trial by fire, CBUT flourished. Once a month Daryl Duke and Mario Prizek produced an enormously ambitious and accomplished musical show—*Parade*—with the ravishing Eleanor Collins and the amazing Don Francks. It was made in a dinky used-car showroom under an eleven-foot ceiling, with extravagant sets (by Doug Stiles) so crammed together that to get from one set-up to the next the cast and crew felt they were—and actually were—fighting their way across a battlefield or an obstacle course. No one watching the show would have guessed.

It was at about this time that Peter MacDonald, an able drama producer who had moved into management and was director of television for British Columbia, made a bold decision. He and Marce Munro determined, rightly, that if CBUT was to make a mark, it would have to be with film. But the government, in a decision that seemed to them entirely sensible, ruled that since the National Film Board was set up to make films and the CBC was to produce television and radio, each should stick to its field. At the CBC we could make film inserts for *Country Calendar*. We could distribute our programs across Canada on the bloody awful kinescopes (there being no national network in place). But we could not make our own film programs. Not even the NFB could do that. They were at the mercy of the CBC, which of course knew what was best for television.

Blissfully ignoring this decree, CBUT began to organize film production. Daryl and Mario stayed with *Parade*, though Daryl was later to make a film about Indians, as people of the First Nations were then called. The second flight of producers, Peter Elkington and Frank Goodship, stayed with news, sports and outside broadcasts. Gene Lawrence, Ron Kelly and I applied for jobs—actually, one job—in what might be called the third flight.

Right after the Commonwealth Games I had thought to apply as an assistant editor and was surprised when Marce now suggested I should apply as a production assistant, thus putting myself in line to become a producer or director. I was flattered, but feared I might be in over my head. I had never expected to become a producer or director. Also, the job would put in me in the production, not the film, department, where Stan was already established as an editor. The two areas were conflicting, not parallel, attractions—film versus television, editing versus production. And I was not all sure of my chances in competition with Gene and Ron: they were both artists and I didn't really know what I was.

Sure enough, as we lined up at the urinals for relief after our interviews, Gene told me that Ron had got the job. But not to worry—there was a second production assistant slot opening up, he said. A month later, he got that one. I held on to my job driving taxi. But third time lucky; another opening came and I got it. We came in, one, two, three, at monthly intervals, and as I recall moved into producing and directing in the same order.

What an extraordinarily intense, exciting and demanding time it was as we learned the craft of television. Nothing in my experience has quite matched it. It was like being in on the invention of the wheel. We were young, and like children we felt that our freshly gained knowledge had just at that very moment, through us, been newly discovered for the world. For we still were the world.

We saw for the first time how moving images are actually put together—on film on a Movieola and in video on a television mixer; we discovered the difference. Moving pictures are constructed one shot at a time, from one point of view or another, and the action is repeated as many times as needed to get it right. Then the shots are edited together so that a single action is reconstructed, as it were, and seems to be taking place in its original

Lindsay Anderson's *Thursday's Children*, an early influence on Allan King

sequence of time—or in a new one if one chooses. Because television takes pictures simultaneously from two, three, even four angles at once, action can be recorded spontaneously, as it happens.

We argued intensely about how to shoot television shows and we had strong views about film. Drama or feature films were out of the question. We were vehemently against what we took to be the National Film Board tradition. We thought of it as the difference between the school of John Grierson and that of Robert Flaherty: to our minds, the former was about social analysis and a burning desire—fuelled by the Great Depression and the Second World War—to change the world. The second school was about actual people caught up in the drama of real life and its conflicts, in stories far from the mundane mendacity of everyday life.

We gloried in the quiet, everyday heroism of Humphrey Jennings's wartime films *A Diary for Timothy* and *Fires Were Started*. The aesthetic credo of *Sequence*, the dominant British film quarterly of the day, was our credo. We had only contempt for the NFB's wartime propaganda news-reel, *Carry On Canada*, which we had come to think of as the beginning and end of the oeuvre of the Board. We were hardly aware of the emerging work of Tom Daly and the directors of NFB's Unit B, among them Colin Low, Roman Kroiter and Wolf Koenig. For me, perhaps the strongest documentary I had seen was Lindsay Anderson's *Thursday's Children*. Its focus and style of exploration combined with its strength in directly dealing with children in difficulty, and offering them real, effective help, became the model for all my work; the "feel" of the film remains vivid in my mind though many of its images have faded.

Films like *Thursday's Children* evoked memories of the turmoil and dis-possession in my own early life. I had lived through my family's loss of our rented home in the Depression. We moved into a single room with an alcove. A month or two later my father and mother separated. My sister and I were boarded out with changing caretakers for a couple of years until my work-ing mother was finally able to afford a home for us. All this made an indeli-ble mark on my view of the world and explains better than anything else why my first independent films felt so personal. *Where Will They Go?* was about hard-core displaced persons in an Austrian refugee camp. *Rickshaw* was about a son inheriting his father's lowly and hopeless profession in Calcutta.

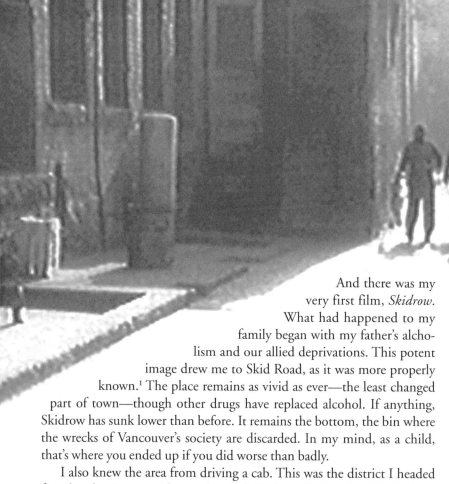

And there was my
very first film, *Skidrow*. *Skidrow*
What had happened to my
family began with my father's alcho-
lism and our allied deprivations. This potent
image drew me to Skid Road, as it was more properly
known.[1] The place remains as vivid as ever—the least changed
part of town—though other drugs have replaced alcohol. If anything,
Skidrow has sunk lower than before. It remains the bottom, the bin where
the wrecks of Vancouver's society are discarded. In my mind, as a child,
that's where you ended up if you did worse than badly.

I also knew the area from driving a cab. This was the district I headed
for when business was slow and I needed a fare. Closing time for the beer
parlours was 11:00 p.m. in those days. And the beer parlours all over town
disgorged their clientele, many of them sodden and staggering, into the
streets. Nowhere in town were they more concentrated than in Skidrow
and especially in front of the Columbia Hotel. The problem was getting
paid or, sometimes, escaping alive. I had one fare who quietly unzipped his
fly, pulled out his penis and emptied his bladder on the front floor of the
cab. When I pulled over to the curb, dragged him out and asked for my
fare, he started to argue and refused to pay, turning his pockets out to show
he had nothing in them. A passing policeman, thinking I was trying to "roll"

the drunk fare for his money, stepped between us. But I did get my money. The fare took off his sodden left shoe and sock, pulled out a limp, well-soaked ten spot and handed it to me. And, despite my protests that I would lose money, having to take the cab back to home base for cleaning, the cop insisted I give full change and take no tip. Other incidents were less funny.

When I finally started thinking about making a film about Skidrow, the person who really introduced me to it was Ben Maartman. Another graduate of the inspiring Earle Birney's creative writing class, Ben was already a well-published short story writer. He had also gone into social work and had acquired an extensive professional familiarity with Skidrow and its culture.

Ben took me on tour over some days and weeks. The geography was fairly simple, bounded as it was by Abbott and Gore Streets on the west and east, and by the waterfront and Pender Street on the north and south. Skidrow's heart was the great anomaly of Victory Square. Research and expression are, in large part, about another set of boundaries—defining what is within the field of discourse: which characters, action, setting, feelings and experience are within it and which are not. Ben had a considerable circle of familiars in the district. The men were certainly not friends, with Ben or each other, in any dictionary sense of the word. The camaraderie of Skidrow regulars was a strong "group marker," best expressed by actions rather than words. For the men who became the focus of our film, or so I discovered in our daily walkabouts, the centre of existence was a shared memory of how they got there.

And so I, the neophyte television producer, realizing that the only way out of producing *Country Calendar*, *Burns' Chuckwagon* and the *Seven O'Clock Show* was to do a film instead, wrote a proposal. We would make a film about the forgotten men of Skidrow. Ben Maartman would write narration and prepare the interviews. And the men would speak on camera.

I gave the proposal to Marce Munro and he said okay.

Notes

1. The name "Skidroad" comes from the track where logs were skidded down from the forest to the water, to be towed to sawmills, hewn into lumber and shipped round the world. It was a place of commerce and bars. As all of Vancouver (then called Gastown) was logged off and wealth accumulated, people moved out of Gastown and Skid Road to Hastings and Granville or Hastings and Main. And the name shifted in popular parlance from Skidroad to Skid Road to Skid Row to Skidrow. Skid Row was, as I recall, an Americanization and was thought to come from Seattle, Vancouver's twin city to the south. Interestingly, when the film was first shown on television, the sharpest criticism in the local newspaper was of my supposed ignorance in using not the "real" name of the district but its American translation. I had hoped the program would spark a discussion of deprivation. In fact "Skidrow" was the name then used by its inhabitants, and who was I to tell them anything different?

Who Has Seen the Wind

Peter Harcourt

Allan King

A Celebration of People

I suppose that the stream that runs through most of the things I respond to is a sense of feeling, of warmth about people, a celebration of people, a sense of humanity. – ALLAN KING*

W. O. Mitchell's *Who Has Seen the Wind* (1947) is a loving evocation of a young boy's consciousness, his growing awareness of the cycle of nature and his gradual recognition of the mystical meaning of life and death. In an oblique way, a pantheistic way, the novel is deeply religious. It is concerned with the forces that animate existence—both nature and people. It is aware of the invisible. It acknowledges the wind.

In 1977, *Who Has Seen the Wind* became a film, adapted by Patricia Watson and directed by Allan King. One of the remarkable achievements of the adaptation is that in this most visual of media they have managed to convey Mitchell's sense of the invisible by moments of speechlessness. The film is full of wide-eyed glances, of silent interrogations—as if trying to come to grips with the significance of things. Largely, of course, these

---

*Except when otherwise noted, all quotations are from *Allan King: An Interview with Bruce Martin* (Ottawa: Canadian Film Institute, 1970).

glances belong to Brian; but they are also received by both his mother and his father and they are shared by Digby, the schoolmaster, in the open-eyed trust with which he greets the world.

In this way, the film implies more than it says. Even the sullen resentment of the Young Ben is conveyed through his body and his eyes. He has almost no lines in the film. Admirers of the novel may be amazed at how little dialogue has been added. For most of Mitchell's imagery, for the interpretative function of his prose, Patricia Watson and Allan King have found visual equivalents.

Who Has Seen the Wind is set in the thirties—a world of hard times, depression and drought. There have been a number of films that depict that period. But with a difference. In Hollywood films like *Bound for Glory*, *Thieves Like Us* and *Bonnie and Clyde*, while the décor is authentic, the thinking is modern. Especially in *Bonnie and Clyde*, which with its New Deal posters and sense of dusty streets is the most meticulous of them all, the gestures are totally contemporary. Although playing characters from the thirties, Warren Beatty and Faye Dunaway speak to our own times. They appeal to our growing suspicion about the processes of the law and the value we now place on individual freedom.

In *Who Has Seen the Wind*, there is no sense of this discrepancy. With his short hair and clear blue eyes, Thomas Hauff as Digby radiates the idealism that seems so characteristically Canadian—particularly in the past. King used eyes in a similar way in his adaptation for television of Barry Broadfoot's *Six War Years*. In that teleplay, it was the same idealistic innocence that projected the Hauff character so willingly into the war. In both *Six War Years* and *Who Has Seen the Wind*, Thomas Hauff seems the incarnation of those times. So it is with everyone in *Who Has Seen the Wind*. There is nothing that seems out of period in their gestures or attitudes.

This is both a distinction and, possibly, a limitation. Audiences might find the film too idealistic, too trusting in the natural processes of life, to be able to believe that that was how it was in those days. They might also be disquieted by the film's lack of protest. Mitchell's pantheism blurs somewhat the social implications of the town's persecution of the Chinese family and of both the Bens. Like the one kitten that dies in the litter or

Who Has Seen the Wind

the runt pig that ought to be destroyed, Nature has its rejects as part of its wholeness. Although certain characters do protest—principally Digby and Miss Thomson—the whole approach is more philosophical than political, urging us toward mysticism and an acceptance of "God's ways."

This idealism in the film, this self-effacing acceptance, is not just fidelity to the original story. There is something of this quality in nearly all of King's work. But in *Who Has Seen the Wind*, Mitchell's prairie world of the thirties is presented with an admirable accuracy. The reconstruction of Arcola, where the film was shot (a reconstruction the townspeople were pleased to accept), the circus posters, auction-sale announcements, period gas-pumps, and Bee Hive Corn Syrup cans combine with those trusting faces, with the expressive speechlessness of their eyes, to create a warmly affirmative experience—an experience rare for our times.

The trust and love within the film is largely carried by Brian Painchaud as Brian. It is his consciousness of the world around him that becomes our consciousness of the film. And by a miracle of casting, there is a sense of tiredness about his eyes—as if he already understands that there will be no satisfactory answers for all the questions he asks about life; as if, finally, the thoughts that most affect him lie too deep for words.

Who Has Seen the Wind is a meditative film. Like the novel it drama-tizes, it contemplates the meaning of human life and the formation of human values. Eldon Rathburn's musical score assists this contemplation. For those of us who know his work, largely for the National Film Board, many of his strategies will sound familiar. But they are effective neverthe-less. Plucked strings and a Jew's harp help to create the boys' excitement as they prepare for their gopher hunt; and when Brian walks off into the prairie to spend the night alone under the stars, a solo horn and widely spaced strings beautifully evoke the landscape's infinite vastness.

Allan King's *Who Has Seen the Wind* goes further than the book in cen-tring this prairie world within Brian's consciousness. In this way, the film becomes a distinguished example of what is really a Canadian genre: films that create the world through the eyes of a young child. Claude Jutra's *Mon Oncle Antoine* and Francis Mankiewicz's *Le Temps d'une chasse* immediately spring to mind; but *Lies My Father Told Me* and *Lions for Breakfast* work in much the same way. If we extend the age to take in adolescents, then the list of films is enormous—in terms of richness and productivity, virtually the Canadian equivalent of the American Western!

If *Who Has Seen the Wind* is characterized by directness and simplicity, these qualities—which are in the novel and can be found in different ways in other films by Allan King—are finally focused through Brian. Most of the world created for us is presented through his eyes—questioning the values of the life and death around him, trying to make sense of it all but drawing no conclusions. Conclusions (if there are any) would belong to another world, a more urban and sophisticated world—a world closer to our own times.

Certainly, in the past at any rate, it's been very much part of my character to be unsure, to be very careful; it's difficult for me to be very forthright emotionally and even forthright in talking in a general way. I'm not sure how much of it is a desire to be covert or how much of it is a simple confusion in my own head about what I feel or what I think.

Who Has Seen the Wind marks a new stage in Allan King's career. Until recently, King has not been known as a director of dramatic features. Like other Canadian filmmakers, he began in documentary. Working out on the West Coast in the late fifties and early sixties, King produced a number of shorts for the CBC that earned him his initial reputation. *Skidrow* (1956), *Rickshaw* (1960), *A Matter of Pride* (1961) and *Bjorn's Inferno or The Devil to Pay* (1964) established the credentials that allowed him to set up production offices in London, England. It was at this time, however, that King began to imagine more challenging projects, moving slowly but surely toward a form that he, more than anybody else, is responsible for developing—the actuality drama.

The actuality drama is a mixture of documentary and fiction. Bypassing the conventional ingredients of script and actors, it uses actual people in actual situations but then shapes the material so that it becomes something more than that—a film by Allan King. The purest example of this way of working is *A Married Couple* (1969). But before that there was an interesting predecessor—virtually an invisible predecessor, because it has been seen by so few people. *Running Away Backwards or Coming of Age in Ibiza* was made for the CBC in 1964. In some ways, it is one of the most interesting films that King has ever made.

It is interesting because it is so naïve and embarrassing—so uncertain about what its values really are. In this way, it takes risks. *Running Away Backwards* tells the story of a group of Canadians "living it up" in Ibiza—trying to "find themselves" away from the insipidities of day-to-day life. Although this ambition seems naïve, it is an experience that more than a handful of Canadians have felt obliged to go through.

Running Away Backwards presents a dilemma for the spectator. Is it a naïve and embarrassing film about a bunch of Canadians sensitive to the uncertainties of their own identities? Or is it a sensitive and uncertain film about a bunch of naïve and embarrassing Canadians who are escaping the demands of maturity by running away to Ibiza? To pose this riddle is to comment on the way King works as a director. The directors we most talk about are those that impose a particular vision of the world upon whatever material they handle. Hitchcock, Bergman, Hawks, Antonioni—even Don Shebib—all have a view of life that is developed in their films. They often have as well a recognizable style—or at least a repertoire of stylistic effects that we learn to associate with their work.

With Allan King, however, these matters are more elusive. There have been, to be sure, some thematic preoccupations. From *Skidrow* through *Warrendale* (1967) to *Come On Children* (1973), King has repeatedly concerned himself with social outcasts, characters who cannot adjust to the conventions of society. This theme is also present in *Running Away Backwards*, even though these pampered middle-class people have melodramatically chosen their outcast state.

But more important than theme is King's attitude as a filmmaker, which is one of self-effacement. Rather than impose himself on his material, Allan King wants the material to speak for itself. Whether it is the immense formality with which he interviews his winos at the time of *Skidrow* or his scrupulous fidelity to the original text in *Who Has Seen the Wind*, as a director King tends to make himself invisible—as if absent from his own films.

One of King's closest affinities is with the French theorist André Bazin. Bazin believed it was the cinema's chief privilege to record directly a pre-existing reality. Thus he preferred the extended takes of William Wyler to the subjective camera of Alfred Hitchcock; and he valued the newsreel quality of the early films of Rossellini over the conceptual editing of Eisenstein. Had he lived to see them, I believe Bazin would also have valued the films of Allan King.

Of course, King is not *actually* absent from his films. But he does stand back, whether through respect or timidity. This is what makes *Running Away Backwards* such a challenging film. Essentially, it is about discontent—the discontent of over a thousand expatriates seeking a "cure" in Ibiza, trying to draw strength from a civilization where there is still some harmony between people and their landscape, where there is still a human pace and scale to life. Yet as the old Spaniard explains toward the end of the film, these Canadians are all spectators, unable to understand. "Words which have disappeared from your dictionaries are still meaningful here," as he explains.

National Archives of Canada / PA212194

On the set of
Running Away Backwards

Throughout the film, the search is presented as both futile and necessary—as a stage one must go through. There is Jake, who leaves at the end because he has seen the limitations of the histrionic self-assertions that this new world has allowed him; while Hank, who has resisted the idleness and sexual freedom that characterize this expatriate community, is left behind—supposedly to do some "grad work" on himself with the young blonde who seems both to attract and frighten him, offering a challenge that, at least in those days, Canadians found hard to deal with on their own soil.

Looked at today, the film contains a lot of nonsense. Yet it is the kind of nonsense that felt real to many people of that fifties generation. The film registers a rejection. But there is no sense of politics and no concern at all with cultural analysis. The characters simply spend their time away, "like children playing in a Roman church," as the old Spaniard explains, and then go home again—no doubt to "earn a buck," having dabbled in sex and art.

The film also registers an immaturity—an immaturity which is part of the embarrassment that the film can cause but is also part of its quality. It is as if Allan King and his associates had the initiative to make explicit some of the adolescent over-assertions that certainly were shared by many Canadians of that generation but which few would have had the courage to express so openly. In this way, the film documents a class of Canadian self-evaders, seeking escape from the moneyed rat-race but finally so dependent on it that inevitably they are drawn back. As the film's title expresses it, these people are "running away backwards," aware of an absence, of something their life has denied them, yet only able to affirm it in the most juvenile of ways.

68

Warrendale

The same attitudes and problems are present in the next three major films that Allan King directed (in between doing bread-and-butter items, largely from London, for the CBC): *Warrendale* (1967), *A Married Couple* (1969) and *Come On Children* (1973). Each film represents a distinguished example of King's early way of working. They are not "just" documentaries but they are not quite dramatic fiction either; and like *Running Away Backwards*, all three films leave us feeling uneasy at the end.

Both *Warrendale* and *Come On Children* concern themselves with adolescents, with young people who feel that they live outside society. *Warrendale* explores the "holding" therapy devised by John Brown for the treatment of emotionally disturbed children—a treatment that (in the film) involves a mixture of extreme caring and something that looks like violence; while *Come On Children* takes a group of "disaffected young people from the suburbs of Toronto" (as the opening title explains) and sets them up on a farm where they are allowed, perhaps encouraged, to "do their own thing."

Of the two films, *Warrendale* is the more disturbing—as much because of the therapy as the filmmaking. The experience of watching it leads us away from the film as film into a discussion of the material it contains.

Yet the film is not neutral. Nor is the fact of filming in such an environment without its effect upon the kids. Young Tony, especially, who is constantly telling everybody to "fuck off!"—a touch of realism that kept the film off the grandmotherly CBC—at one point looks directly at the camera and asks, "Why do I swear all the time?" An answer is not hard to find. Like other people in the film (though to a lesser degree), he is aware of his "performance."

The film is remarkable for the environment it creates—both topographical and psychological. The Warrendale clinic looks indeed like a warren of dwellings placed in a mud-and-rubble wasteland—a suburban nightmare that, in itself, can't help but increase the sense of isolation that all the children feel. In a way not unlike the attitudinizing adults in *Running Away Backwards*, the kids are cut off from their everyday lives—from their actual homes, which one can only hope would be more humane. While I lack the competence fully to discuss the implications of this therapy, it is disturbing, to say the least.

I can see its virtues—the virtues of confrontation. The kids are not allowed to retreat into themselves. When they shout or get violent, they are shouted at in return and held firmly by caring arms. But sometimes this holding involves as many as three adults at a time for just one child. And the kids are expected to verbalize everything. Tony must explain why he resents Terry's bad breath, and Carol must rationalize her resentment of

Walter—the fact that she misses him because he is rarely there. Is this treatment loving force or emotional rape? This question is left unanswered.

The film finds its centre in the death of Dorothy, the cook—one of those "happy accidents" in filmmaking that allow filmmakers to shape their material toward a climax. But even this, considering the nature of the event and the public way it is announced, with all the kids gathered together and the camera ready to roll, is somewhat disturbing.

Come On Children

But as a film, *Warrendale* is important largely because it leaves us with all these problems. It confronts us directly with the perhaps questionable validity of the therapy and the troublesome ethics of filmmaking. Once again King has taken on a project that more cautious people would have shied away from.

Come On Children is organized in much the same way, except that there is no "happy accident." One of the girls has a baby, but this isn't dwelt on; one of the guys shoots up speed. Another lad, John Hamilton, really becomes the "star" of the film. Through his songwriting, he is also a kind of choric commentator. He is constantly playing the guitar, entertaining us with stories and his unfocused charm. A small confrontation occurs when the parents come up for a day. But even this is low-key—a sad but not basically an angry presentation of the generation gap of which these kids are so aware.

There were a number of films about young people made at the end of the sixties, before the Youth Generation gave way to what Tom Wolfe has called the Me Generation: Mort Ransen's *Christopher's Movie Matinée* and Jacques Godbout's *Kid Sentiment*, both made in 1968; and Claude Jutra's *Wow* made the following year. In the context of these films, *Come On Children* is admirable both because of the respect it brings to the kids and because of the quiet rhythm that gradually establishes itself as they sit around and talk and sing and do not much at all. And if the sense of intrusion seems less here than in *Warrendale*, it is nevertheless made explicit at a couple of points in the film.

During an early sequence while two of the boys are eating breakfast, one of them becomes increasingly impatient with the fact he is being filmed, an impatience that becomes anger before our eyes. "You're fuckin' the shit outta me, man," he finally screams, putting his hand up before the camera. And toward the end of the film, as the kids are getting ready to leave, one of them is directly interviewed by King himself—a rare disruption for an Allan King film. "What are you going back to?" we hear King ask from behind the camera; and then there is a whole series of questions concerning what he is going to do, what he would like to do if he went away, what he would do there and so on. To each of these questions, in a pleasantly smiling but ultimately hopeless way, the young lad replies "Nothing." Nothing in the world as he has known it. "Maybe get with whatever's happening elsewhere," as he finally explains.

Like so many of King's films, *Come On Children* presents people without a future, without a culture to sustain them, with no clear idea of what they exist in the world to do. The film starts off with John singing the well-known Dylan song which seems to sum up the feeling of them all:

> . . . I'm walkin' down that long lonesome road, babe,
> Where I'm bound I can't tell . . .

Miraculously, however, King's discreet direction combines with the editing skills of Arla Saare to give this film in which nothing happens a gently reflective rhythm and distinct shape of its own. It becomes a quiet kind of drama—a drama of nice kids who have a real respect for one another but who feel there is nothing to do and nowhere to go. It's no wonder the film hasn't been seen. It would be too much like an accusation.

Some of the critics . . . felt that *A Married Couple* had no imagination or that it was somehow dull. I'm a little puzzled by the expectations for fantasy in film, for mythmaking; it seems that if you can give people a comfortable fantasy or myth, it is easier for them to accept. If you say what you feel directly or show them the world as you experience it, this seems to cause difficulties.

Of all the films of this period, *A Married Couple* represents King's most dramatic achievement. Although—like many other distinguished Canadian films of that time—it hasn't been a great commercial success, its influence has been considerable, most obviously on the American television series *An American Family* but also on the parliamentary documentation done in Britain by Roger Graef (one of the old team of Allan King Associates when they were based in London).

It is not exactly an agreeable film, unless you enjoy listening to people shouting at one another for the better part of an hour and a half. It is not a film that makes you wish you were married! But what is extraordinary is that the couple King found to consent to such a project, Billy and Antoinette Edwards, are both natural performers. They bring an energy to everything they do that makes for interesting material on the screen.

Seen nowadays, several years after it was made, the film seems like a study of oppression—largely of the man over the woman but also of all members of the family by the structures of family life. As a family, the Edwardses quantify everything. Nearly all their squabbles concern money and the acquisition of material goods—a pair of forty-dollar shoes; a new shag rug; a gas stove for their remodelled kitchen, a washer and dryer, a new hi-fi! In characteristic fashion, Billy offers the classical male argument: since he makes most of the money, he has most of the rights—an argument that Antoinette strives constantly to resist.

As the Edwardses depict it for us in the edited version of their lives which we have in this film, married life is a struggle for dominance with all the cards stacked in favour of the male. Even their sex life becomes part of this battle. Antoinette tries desperately to defend her right, when she feels like it, to sleep in her own bed. Talk between the Edwardses seems like thrust and counter-thrust, with Antoinette's suggestions becoming more and more preposterous the more aggressively they are resisted. Like their opening argument about the harpsichord, for example, a scene that reads so tersely in transcript that it seems hard to believe it never was written:

ANTOINETTE: Where do you think we should put the harpsichord? Over there?

BILLY: The harpsichord. I don't know. The same place we're gonna put the rock band. What harpsichord?

A Married Couple: Post-Rough-Cut Format

HARPSICHORD DISCUSSION

WAKE UP

BREAK FAST

DRIVE TO WORK (ARRIVAL AT ESPLANADE) →

CAFE DE LA PAIX ←———— PSYCH?

SUPPER PRE-CAR FIGHT

CAR FIGHT

EXIT ANTOINETTE

EXT RECORDING STUDIO

HOUSEWORK

RECORDING SESSION

HOME SCENE WITH BOART NEAR DINNER

Horsey?
~~Taking off work clothes?~~
Other?

NEW REGIME

~~mechanical~~ PHOTONITE INCLUDING BEDREJECTION + RED SHIRT

DANCE CLASS ⌐ PSYCH

MARTIN GOODMAN

Poss HORSEY WITH MERTON AND BOGART ?

SUPPER WITH KITCHEN AND RECORD DISSCUSSION

~~NEXT~~ HI FI DANCING 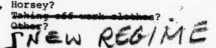 + SKI BOOTS · REJECT

~~PARTY MONTAGE (THE SHOTS)~~

TENDERNESS   BY ITSELF?

THROWOUT ~~NIGHT~~ ; NIGHT

SUPPER

BEDFIGHT

COUCH FIGHT

TITLES

ANTOINETTE: That I'm gonna buy.

BILLY: You're not gonna buy a harpsichord.

ANTOINETTE: Oh yes I am—with part of my money.

BILLY: Oh no, you're not gonna buy a harpsichord.

ANTOINETTE: Yes, I'm gonna buy a musical instrument.

BILLY (shouting): You're not gonna buy a harpsichord. And the reason you're not buying a harpsichord is because the harpsichord is a selfish instrument just for you. The money's gonna go to buying the things we absolutely need. What do we need a goddamn harpsichord for?

ANTOINETTE: How can I study voice again if I don't have a musical instrument?

BILLY: You don't need a harpsichord. I'll get you a harmonica.

If there is rarely the sense of a genuine conversation between the two of them, rarely the sense of speech as exchange, the film is not without its moments of tenderness. Billy is often presented playing with their son, Bogart, or fondling their dog, Merton. There is a lovely moment when all four of them are sitting on the floor together, testing out their new hi-fi and exchanging kisses with one another (even with Merton), while listening to that old Beatles song "Maria." Right after this scene, Billy and Antoinette are alone together, dancing to "I'd love to turn you on . . . ," Antoinette all wrapped around Billy as they move together, the image fractured by the bevelled glass of the French doors that the cameraman, Richard Leiterman, is shooting through. It is a most effective moment, I would argue, because the distance both suggests reticence on the part of the crew concerning this intimacy and, through the splitting up of the image, the scene also suggests the fragmentation of their lives.

A sadder, even more tender moment occurs after a party sequence toward the end of the film. Antoinette has been flirting with some guy in a red shirt, which (as the film is fictionalized in the editing) seems to have led to a sort of squabble between the Edwardses once they got home. After the party, the film picks them up in close-up, cuddling on the sofa. Antoinette is crying and talking quietly to Billy—possibly the most tender talk in the film. But we can't hear what they are saying. A record (one of Sarastro's arias

from *The Magic Flute*) erases their speech. Although the scene actually happened this way when they were shooting, this effect again suggests reticence on the part of the filmmakers. It also forces us to deal purely visually with the significance of the scene.

A Married Couple

It is not an encouraging moment. Antoinette seems really disturbed, as if trying to reach Billy. But his face is largely turned away from her—as if, as elsewhere in the film, he is rejecting whatever she has to offer him. The scene ends with a dissolve to Antoinette alone in her own bed, cuddling her pillow. Then we cut to Billy, still downstairs, finishing off a drink and patting the dog.

A Married Couple is a highly distinctive film. There is nothing like it anywhere in the world. It is a frightening experience. Like the other films of this "documentary" period, *A Married Couple* is also a film about exiles, about people cut off from a culture that might sustain them. While there is no political analysis in any of King's films, they cry out for a political interpretation. They are about alienation. They present the separation of the individual from culture. Unless we are deeply pessimistic about life and accept all these problems as an unalterable aspect of "human nature," King's films all suggest the need for social change.

Whether King himself is aware of this need, I do not know. Certainly, his characters aren't. Antoinette and Billy see nothing wrong with the institution of marriage as it exists, with their pursuit of the perfect home. The problems are all internalized. Both Billy's dominance and Antoinette's resentment are ritualized in the routines of their marriage. At one point during one of their fights, Billy is explicit about this situation. "The framework isn't the problem," he cries out at her. "The laws of society are not the problem in this marriage. The problem is you and me . . . What we don't know is whether we really hate one another or not."

Like both *Warrendale* and *Come On Children*, like most of the early work of Allan King, *A Married Couple* is a film that, in spite of the fine shape that King and Arla Saare finally evolved for it, leads us away from the film as film to talk about the problems it contains—the problems of marriage and of unfulfilment in the contemporary world.

Although the film ends tenderly, it also ends with non-achievement—with Antoinette and Billy seeking the creature comforts of touching one another, of holding one another. Nothing is resolved. We know that the next day, fresh squabbles will begin. The Edwardses are trapped within their own image of themselves: middle-class consumers whose life values are as empty and non-sustaining as the silly Heinz commercials Billy has to supervise. As the film presents them, the Edwardses' lives are as barren of human sustenance as the wasteland setting of *Warrendale* and as hopeless of a future as the end of *Come On Children*. It is not a comforting view of the world.

I'd done most of what I wanted to do in documentary simply as a technical form. I didn't see it shifting very much from there. Also, I had always used documentary essentially as a dramatic form. I've done essay films, but I've always been interested in stories about people. It was never practical in Vancouver where I started—to do dramatic work. We didn't have the budgets. We didn't think we had the experience to work in that manner. So one made films about real people and told a story about them.

In essence, the form of *Warrendale* is a dramatic structure; and with *A Married Couple*, it is directly a dramatic structure with two central characters. The fact that they're documentaries, for me, has always been coincidental. That was economically where I could work.

Using actors and scripts has more control in many respects and also allows for a range of experience that is beyond the scope of individuals who are playing themselves. Also, I began to feel that I wanted that kind of control. I wanted to be able to work more directly in a dramatic form, with actors.

– ALLAN KING, in conversation with Peter Harcourt (1977)

Since the dissolution of his offices in London and of his Toronto company after *Come On Children*, Allan King has been working more than ever with television. But now with a difference. Since 1974, he has been increasingly involved with drama, involving real scripts and real actors. In some ways this is more conventional work than he has done in the past.

There are several reasons for his switch to drama, both financial and practical. Financially, in spite of their distinction, King's actuality dramas didn't make much money; and practically, through John Hirsch and the revitalization of television drama at the CBC, all of a sudden work in filmed drama became a possibility. There are other factors too that may have influenced him: his increased association with Patricia Watson and his admiration for Toronto's little theatre—for directors like Paul Thompson and Martin Kinch and for playwrights like Carol Bolt, two of whose plays he has filmed.

In fact, his version of *Red Emma* (1976) has much of the old King quality about it. Helped by the fine camera work of Edmund Long, King made what at times looks like a documentary of Kinch's stage production, at other times like a film version of the play, with Kinch directing the actors and King his film crew. Kinch worked with King again for Rick Salutin's *Maria* (1977), a film about a young woman in a clothing factory who tries to organize a union. This time, however, Kinch is the dialogue coach and King is the director. It is as if, by these means, King has been training himself for the different challenges of dealing with actors.

The most innovative of these programs is *Six War Years* (1975), a video adaptation by Norman Klenman of Barry Broadfoot's oral history of the Second World War. Working directly on tape, King was able to superimpose close-ups in colour of the faces speaking directly to us over black-and-white newsreel footage of the war; and he also had a handful of actors play out a variety of roles. Apparently influenced by Paul Thompson's work with Theatre Passe Muraille, *Six War Years* might be described as a piece of "epic" television—a Brechtian combination of direct statement and dramatic recreation that simultaneously moved and informed us. Its achievement still represents one of the most original hours of television that I have seen anywhere in the world.

Less satisfactory, to my mind, is King's direction of *Baptizing* (1975), drawn from the story by Alice Munro. My own misgivings about this film centre on the music. While the story connects young Del's dreams of romantic love with listening to opera, the decision to run operatic music over her later scenes of lovemaking has disquieting results. First of all, it gives to these sequences an Elvira Madiganish sort of lyricism which is a cliché, to say the least. Secondly, the continued use of this music might imply that the reality of making love is still wrapped up with Del's dreams, without increased maturity—thus denying the point of the original story.

Who Has Seen the Wind

Nevertheless, *Baptizing* provided a fine experience for its viewers within the opiate world of television. It certainly offered an excellent training ground for the greater challenges of *Who Has Seen the Wind*.

It is difficult at this stage to see where Allan King is going. Since *Who Has Seen the Wind*, King has already made a film version of Carol Bolt's *One Night Stand*, and I assume that he will go on working for the CBC. But he wants to make theatrical features; and even if this means he is working in a more conventional mode, Allan King's artistic presence can still be felt.

The exact nature of this presence is hard to characterize. It has to do with innocence and also with naïveté—initially about the expected characteristics of the medium he was working in and, throughout his life, about the complexities of existence, especially when seen from a socio-political point of view. Arguably, these characteristics are what make his films so unmistakably Canadian, speaking from and to an Anglo-Saxon middle-class culture that was at one time too dominant, but which has become increasingly uncertain of itself since the Second World War. Possibly also related to this is King's lack of self-assertion: in his documentary days, his respect for the reality he was filming; now, in drama, his respect for the original text.

Thinking about King's achievement, I remember Keats's notion of "negative capability"—an openness to experience that Keats believed was essential to the receptivity of the artist. This openness Allan King has in abundance—almost to a fault. Before *Who Has Seen the Wind*, King's major films were about rejects—misfits within established society. But this subject matter is never analysed. The situations are simply presented, always with King's sensitivity and respect, but there is little in the films to betray his personal attitude.

Perhaps King's work on *Red Emma* and *Maria* will lead to a more direct awareness of the political issues that form a submerged dimension in all his work. But if his films present characters with no culture to sustain them—culture in the anthropological sense of shared values and conventions—then this could well explain both King's attraction to and the achievement of *Who Has Seen the Wind*.

Who Has Seen the Wind is a recreation of a past time when society was not vitiated by generation gaps and battles between the sexes, a world where—as Helen sings at the beginning of *Red Emma*—"all their lies were true." People believed in things: in the process of nature, in the continuity of human life, in the necessity of self-sacrifice—as they did as well, more grimly, in *Six War Years*. The dominant male-centred culture had not yet been challenged or made aware of its increasing inability to nurture its own children.

Furthermore, the formal tidiness of fiction must now be attractive to King because fiction provides a stronger sense of order than is possible with documentary, struggling after the event to find an order in the editing. Finally, the extraordinary feeling of both sincerity and wholeness that characterizes every frame of *Who Has Seen the Wind* is all the more impressive because these qualities are the characteristics of a past that still had a strong sense of active community values, values that have virtually vanished from the suburban sprawl of our increasingly urbanized world—the setting of so many of King's previous films.

Who Has Seen the Wind complements Allan King's previous work, as if rounding it off and bringing it to an end. But in its scope, in its director's newly achieved confidence in working with actors, and in the many extraordinary beauties throughout the length of its fictionalized form, *Who Has Seen the Wind* is also a beginning.

1978

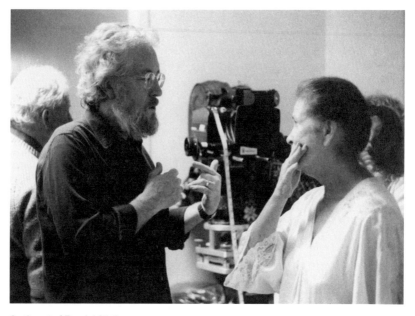

On the set of *Termini Station*

Blaine Allan, Seth Feldman, Peter Harcourt

Allan King Plus Three

An Interview

We met on March 4, 2002, in Allan King's Toronto living room, where we sat around a large coffee table beneath brightly coloured Mediterranean art. Blaine Allan had helped bring an archival collection of King's work to Queen's University. Peter Harcourt, one of the founders of Canadian film studies, has known King for more than thirty years. I've known Allan King for almost that long; I had invited him to the Grierson Film Seminar in 1984, where a discussion of Who's in Charge? *had ended in a fistfight. The atmosphere was more peaceful on the day of this interview. We had coffee and began to talk.*

PETER HARCOURT: You once said in an interview that you hated making films.

ALLAN KING: I find it terrifying. Somebody once asked: "If you were given a million dollars what film would you make?" And I said, "I would put the money in the bank and I would never make another one."

PETER HARCOURT: Do you still hate it?

ALLAN KING: I tell you, my letters home from Estonia during the last weeks of making *The Dragon's Egg* were piteous and pitiable. Documentaries are terrifying. Television episodes are a piece of cake because they are so contrived. It's work to a pattern. Original work, like a feature, I found difficult although less so later on when I got more skilful. But the difficulty there is interpreting. You're always looking over your shoulder wondering, What does the writer think? That's why I have always had the writer on set if at all possible.

SETH FELDMAN: But filmmaking must offer you some pleasures and satisfaction?

ALLAN KING: Oh, it's discovery. Doing a documentary, particularly as we got freer and the equipment got lighter and lighter and more able to do those things that you always saw, and thought, Oh if I could just capture that now, but you never could because the equipment was too cumbersome—it was being able to explore territory. A universe of discourse, if you will. I read a lot but I never quite discover as much as I do in the course of making a film because the people you film teach you all sorts of stuff; the stuff they give you— it's spontaneous, it comes out of nowhere, you get extraordinary subtexts. Audiences tell you all sorts of things about your films. You learn things thirty years later that you never knew.

SETH FELDMAN: For example?

ALLAN KING: I've just discovered something about *A Married Couple* that never occurred to me before. It was about the moment when Billy and Antoinette have been down in Maine at Eastport, and she has been flirting with a guy and playing with her tassels, fairly close to her genital area. And there is a sense that there may or may not have been an affair. There wasn't an affair. But at any rate, there she is sitting on his lap and there is an aria, a bass aria from *The Magic Flute*. And she is crying. It seemed to sum up the whole feeling of where they were and her feelings. And I think it affected people very strongly. What I just learned from Richard [Leiterman] is that what Antoinette was crying about was that we were almost done filming, and Richard and Chris [Wangler] would be going. They wouldn't be a fixture in the house any more.

And talking to Richard, I thought: Well, you know, does that mean that I have committed an offence in ethics or truth and so on, by using feelings for one apparent thing when it's another? Does it mean that Antoinette didn't have those feelings? But what I finally realized, of course, was that the tears were tears of loss and they only come because one has experienced many losses and some thoroughly profound ones and the distance between her and Billy was partly that as well. So that it was perfectly appropriate.

And there is another question that some people raise: Are they acting? And it sort of begs the question, because even if they were acting, where did the stuff come from? You know, it's like dreams. They are your dreams. The action in the dream is yours because you have remembered the dream and you have created the dream. And the feelings are what you may act with or pretend with. So they are valid. Feelings in a sense are unchallenged. Unchallengeable. But they are often surprising.

BLAINE ALLAN: Okay, but you're there as well. What role does making a film, especially a film meant for broadcast, play in that kind of therapeutic situation?

ALLAN KING: One gets caught in a bind and I discovered that nowhere more acutely than with *Warrendale*, because my objective in the film, and the goal of the film, was to explore the experience of being a child. *Warrendale* turned out to be an extraordinarily vivid location because the children's freedom of expression was the priority. Kids were encouraged to express their feelings as long as they didn't hurt themselves, the place, the property or other kids. But the object of the film wasn't to make a statement about treatment. I happened to have views rising out of it, but the film wasn't designed or edited to express those views. A film always has to be edited to reflect and make meaningful the experience that you have recorded. Just as if you write a book. You imagine all the experience and express all the feelings in your text and then you shape it into a meaning. But if you start to shape it into a didactic meaning, or good guys versus bad guys, you end up with a very trivial piece of work.

I had a similar notion with *A Married Couple*, that if you could look at a marriage in conflict with sufficient acuity, care and attention, you might be able to discover reasons why marriages get into difficulty. The film suggests a number of them. Billy and Antoinette said their reason for going into the film was to see if they could resolve the problems in their marriage. They looked at all the footage, swore that they would never do those things again and of course did. As we all do. Because you can have all the insight in the world but it doesn't mean that you are going to change.

BLAINE ALLAN: In films like *Come On Children* and *Who's in Charge?* aren't you putting people in a contrived, stressful situation just to see how they cope with it?

ALLAN KING: *Come On Children* and *Who's in Charge?* didn't put anybody anywhere. This is fundamentally important. *Come On Children* came about because we were asked to make a film about teenagers and drugs. I was interested in young people and what they were feeling. We did a huge research project. We talked to four or five hundred teenagers across the suburban belt of Toronto. We found they all wanted certain things. They wanted to get away from the city. They hated the regimentation of school. There was no place for them to be in society. They couldn't sit in shopping malls; they couldn't sit in coffee shops and so on. And they kept saying that it would be great to just get away to a place in the country. Then we said, "Well, maybe it would," and we invited about ten people who wanted to do that. In that sense it was inviting people to do what they said they wanted to do. And explore what would come from it. And what did come from it was three or four people who really discovered something. John Hamilton was one, the boy who got off speed—which at that time everybody said you couldn't do.

With *Who's in Charge?* we invited thirty people from all walks of life and all parts of the country to explore their experience of being employed and unemployed. We made a very clear structure for it, defining time, place and space. We were very careful never to invade the private space that they had. The only time we filmed was actually

Allan King in
Who's in Charge?

National Archives of Canada / PA212193

during the conference, the part that was prescribed for the task that they had undertaken to do: to explore their experience in front of cameras. So all of the things that they undertook, they clearly and rationally undertook to a very clear and precise prospectus. What perhaps they didn't understand is that it is difficult to explore. One does try to avoid it. But one earns one's independence by exploring. One gets one's authority, as it were. You can't give people authority. You just can't do it. And they only find out by getting mad, asking questions, like, Why do you guys get up at a certain time, when somebody's talking, and walk out? Well, how do you find that out? Because they give you an answer? You nod, and you're sceptical and that's bullshit. But if you dig, you realize that time is finite. There's only so much of it.

There needs to be a boundary between work and play. The boundary is quite precise. It's one hour. And the hour is up. And if you watch your clock, and you know that, you'll discover it. We respect work. A precise schedule for work is a respect for work, not disrespect for the people doing it. It is a boundary that says whoever wants to continue talking is welcome to do that, but we don't regard that now as work because we are out of work time. So all of that stuff is stuff to be explored, and you only learn it if you explore it and discover it for yourself.

SETH FELDMAN: Many the critiques of *Who's in Charge?* were ideologically based. And maybe not just the ideology of that film but the way you dismiss ideology in a lot of your work.

ALLAN KING: I think ideology, like religion, is seriously flawed. It tends to be blind. The Platonic notion of taking an abstract as real is terrible bunk. Abstractions are useful tools for thinking. They end up as a part of particular language that you use as a way of looking at the world. Ideologies are fundamentally an avoidance of the hard work of tackling reality. And I am fundamentally interested in exploring reality. One finds that it's full of contradictions and all the values in it are human. And therefore, being human, they tend to be full of tensions between various notions of what is good and what is valuable. Life is about working out resolutions between those tensions and those conflicts so that you can live longer, hurt people less, get more pleasure and do all of things people want to do.

When we were making *Who's in Charge?*, I was very much affected by the way people avoid work if possible. One of the key ways of doing that is to nominate a couple of people to write a bible or a constitution or a set of rules so you don't have to think. So in the end, I didn't share the perspective of those people in *Who's in Charge?* who wanted to destroy the conference or drive a tank to Ottawa and blow the place up. I think that's a mistake. I spent enough time in logging camps with the IWA [International Word-workers of America] and the communists, and the social democrats and I find myself increasingly a social democrat. But there is no language any more for it because I do find the market is useful in lots of things. It just isn't an answer to all sorts of things like what's good in art. The world is much more complicated than ideology.

PETER HARCOURT: You have always been concerned with outcasts, from the alcoholics in *Skidrow* to the unemployed in *Who's in Charge?*, the mother and daughter in *Termini Station* and the Russians in *The Dragon's Egg*. What does that mean for you?

ALLAN KING: Well, as I became a little more self-aware, a process that I suppose started with *Warrendale*, I began to call myself Little Orphan Allan. That was really about my parents splitting when I was six and the extraordinarily traumatic effect of that and then moving to two or three other families to live for the next two or three years, and then my family getting together again and then splitting again. And then my mother remarried and I thought that was the ultimate betrayal, you see, because we had

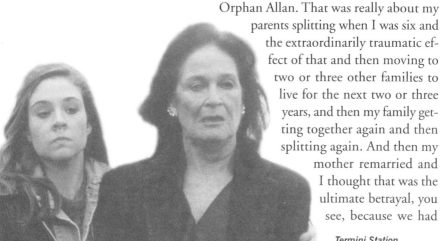

Termini Station

finally gotten back together, at least my mother, my sister and I did.

SETH FELDMAN: Not to psychoanalyse—well, okay, to psychoanalyse—how did those early childhood experiences shape your approach to the world around you?

ALLAN KING: As a kid, I had the notion that if you thought hard enough, explored enough, we would probably find the answer to all the world's problems and people would be happy instead of miserable. Or so I thought as a child. I spent all my time at university studying philosophy. It started with Greek philosophy, the earliest of Greeks, and it went almost up to modern times. I found that extraordinarily valuable.

PETER HARCOURT: Didn't your background also have something to do with you going into documentary? I remember when he interviewed you in the 1970s, Bruce Martin suggested that to you the idea of writing fiction, when you were a young man, was equivalent to telling a lie—that you couldn't actually invent something.

ALLAN KING: Well, it was certainly my theory that Canadians' difficulty writing fiction well into their history can be traced to the Ulster and Scots background that made banking and insurance our first and primary industries. For accountants, bankers and insurance people, fiction was close to lying and much disapproved of. So I think there was that repression.

But also there always are very good vernacular storytellers. I was never one. In fact, in Vancouver I was the only one out of our group that had no talent. Stan [Fox] was a good cameraman. Rolph [Blakstad] was a great painter. He got an Emily Carr scholarship. Gene Lawrence was unquestionably the most talented of us. He had the most imagination. Extraordinary vision. I didn't know what I was doing. I didn't have the vision or the eye that Gene did.

SETH FELDMAN: Was there a West Coast school of filmmaking in the late 1950s, some common aesthetic that brought you all together?

ALLAN KING: The name—the "West Coast school"—came, I gather, from Unit B at the National Film Board after we began making films in Vancouver. We didn't think of ourselves as a school. I made *Skidrow*, and the Film Board was kind of struck with it. It was different than the way they were doing things. I remember taking *Rickshaw* to the Montreal festival and being interviewed by Claude Jutra who was then very young. And he referred to the West Coast film school and I was dumbfounded, because we used to fight like cats and dogs. It was one of the great virtues of the place. We used to argue so much we really learned a lot about film from the arguing. We certainly learned who we were and what we liked that was different from each other. And I always enjoyed debating. I am insufferable in my need to teach and explain the truth of everything.

SETH FELDMAN: But out of that nonexistent West Coast school you get a very particular kind of *cinéma-vérité*—which you then brought to England.

ALLAN KING: I didn't go to England to bring *cinéma-vérité* to the English. I went to England because my wife wouldn't come back to Canada from Ibiza. And I found Ibiza impossible to work in over the long haul because Franco made it very difficult to bring film in and out. I eventually ended up setting up shop in England. I started doing work from there for the CBC. Mostly interviews and public affairs shows for Ross McLean, a lot of them with Douglas Leiterman. They paid for the documentaries we did—like *Rickshaw* and *Where Will They Go?* And docudramas or essay-dramas like *Joshua* and *Running Away Backwards*—a number of films before *cinéma-vérité* actually got going. Although we were getting lighter and lighter equipment, I guess the real break was with the adaptation of the Auricon that Albert [Maysles] and his brother [David] made. I phoned Albert to find out about this camera. So we had long talks and he was very generous, we hit it off very well. So I got one. And that's really what sort of triggered *cinéma-vérité* in Britain.

SETH FELDMAN: Looking back now, where does your work from the early 1960s into the 1970s fit into this period of *cinéma-vérité* and the ideas about documentary film?

ALLAN KING: A lot of *cinéma-vérité* hinged on the drama that came from the event. You have to find a sufficient tension within a work to sustain the length of what you want to explore. But for me, it's always been about people, my fascination has always been with individual people or individual people within the group—personal actuality drama, if you will.

SETH FELDMAN: Your films also seem to be more sympathetic to institutions than most of the *cinéma-vérité* from that period—beginning with the Salvation Army in *Skidrow*, and in the later films all those psychologists and institutions. Do you think they really do help? Do you include them with some ironic intent? Are they part of a dramatic conflict?

ALLAN KING: It's both. It is part of the conflict. I have always been interested in groups or organizations that do in fact try to solve problems—from the first strikes I used to get into and union activity when I worked in the logging camps. The key for *Skidrow* was a social worker and writer, Ben Maartman. I was disconcerted when I discovered that he felt there was really nothing you could do about people on skidrow. I have come to the conclusion, after many years, that I agree. I don't think you can help people who don't want to change. It is very hard to have a homeless person stay in a home because they don't *want* to stay in a home. I am convinced now that most people get the result that they want. Or that they emotionally need. The real difficulty is between what one says, what one rationally wants, and what one is driven to by need. And the drive or the need for things that in a sense are perverse, or don't gratify what ordinary people find gratifying, is a kink in character, which produces an outcome that is, for most people, unacceptable. But it *is* needed by the person who feels it.

So what do you do for those people? You can try to ensure that they don't get hurt, that they get fed, that they get cared for in various ways. But respect their need for what they want. And don't get into a huge moral fuss about it. It took me many years to work through all of that. With *Warrendale*, for example, I learned that you could work with kids and help, particularly if they were young and had the flexibility to break through. I think people can work through problems and solve them. Emotional problems particularly. If they want to. But our tenacity is really daunting to overcome. We hold to our neuroses with great tenacity because they are part of our very identity. The most terrifying thing of all for most people is to lose their identity. It's the hardest, most painful aspect of schizophrenia.

PETER HARCOURT: You once said that what took you to documentary was a wish to explore your own thoughts and feelings—that you felt uncertain about—through the thoughts and feelings of other people. I want to know whether that's changed over the years. Are you still uncertain of your thoughts and feelings?

ALLAN KING: I am particularly surprised by my feelings, because I often think that I know them and then I get caught by surprise and am dumbfounded. Actually, I burst into tears very easily. But I also get angry over some things I thought I had full management over. I am always surprised by my feelings—perhaps because for many years I was a very closed person and hid my feelings even from myself.

PETER HARCOURT: When you began to make dramatic films during the 1970s, it seems to me, there was a considerable change in your approach. For instance, you relied a lot on adaptations.

ALLAN KING: Well, there were two reasons for that. First of all I went broke doing documentaries. It was impossible to fund them. All of the

money in Canada then was going into features through the Canadian Film Development Corporation or CBC television drama. So I started doing drama at the CBC. And the principal series like *To See Ourselves* and *Performance* were virtually all adaptations. Patricia Watson, to whom I was married then, liked doing adaptations, so she started doing adaptations and I directed them. And we formed a relationship with David

Maria

Baptizing

Peddie. That's how I learned to do drama because I had no idea how to direct actors at that point. And I learned a lot by doing.

PETER HARCOURT: You were also working with the theatre director Martin Kinch?

ALLAN KING: That was sort of a second phase. Before that I did a *Bird in the House, Can I Count You In* and other stories for CBC's *Anthology* series. So I had been doing hour-long drama. After that I started to get involved with *Who Has Seen the Wind*. Before I could get it financed I had to stop and wait for the Saskatchewan government to have an election, so I went into the CBC to work with John Hirsch. John was very daring, very innovative, lots of stuff going on; he would take chances, had good taste, so it was an exciting time. That's when I made *Maria*, and *Red Emma* and *Baptizing*. I shot *Red Emma* and *Baptizing* back to back. I started a thirteen-part series for the CBC. I did another thing on Canadian theatre.

Working with Martin Kinch on projects like *Red Emma*, I also learned more about directing actors. It's not about directing actors either. It's about how do you work. Martin made it legitimate not to direct. He was the first person I had heard say: "You must let the actor discover the truth about their character because then they own it and if they don't own it, after opening night they will do what they bloody well please anyway. So you better make sure that they own it."

I learned more after doing *Who's in Charge?* and actually after going to the Tavistock Institute's Leicester conference. Most people get into difficulty and do poor work because they try to tell other people what to do. Very few people accept the fact that, practically speaking, authority always comes from your role in relation to a task. Therefore, one has to be precise, and think clearly about what the task is. The director's task is really to manage, and to realize the concept. And hold to what the concept is. But it isn't to design the set. It isn't to light the set. It isn't to act the performance. It isn't to write the script.

SETH FELDMAN: Much of what you've done since the mid-1980s has been television, some anthology shows, some episodes for ongoing series. What attracted you to that kind of work?

ALLAN KING: Money. I couldn't make a living doing the work I wanted to do. Episodic television is an easy, undemanding way to make money. And it had other compensations.

I always enjoyed running a show well, shooting it on time, on budget. I like planning, thinking the show through. When I began it was very hard for me to be really visual, much less write down on paper what the show was going to look like. I'd make a shot list but it was laborious. But doing an episode I could write a shot list like you'd write a script. It didn't mean that I would follow the shot list but at least everybody knew what we were about. It also gave me and everybody else much more freedom to invent. You have a structure underneath you that you can fall back on. Thinking it through on paper is a way of processing the script, in terms of feelings, who's doing what, what's significant, what's not significant. I found that gratifying.

Sometimes the scripts were fun. The *Alfred Hitchcock Presents* episodes were a delight to do. On *Road to Avonlea*, I sometimes thought Kevin [Sullivan] was too infatuated with subplots. Not trusting the audience enough, not crediting them with an attention span. But he provided splendid resources, he never skimped on his shows. The sets were excellent, the schedules better than other series. And working with Christopher Lloyd, Diane Keaton, Stockard Channing, Jackie Burroughs, Zack Bennett, Cedric Smith and the other key actors, that was a real joy.

PETER HARCOURT: What brought you back to documentary, specifically *The Dragon's Egg*?

ALLAN KING: I became interested in ethnic identity and conflict in the middle of Czechoslovakia, which was posing as nineteenth-century Prussia in a mini-series I was doing, *By Way of the Stars*. And I suddenly found myself in a rage, thinking, Why am I making this film about Prussia? What is this film about? It's about rehabilitating Prussia! Why do I want to rehabilitate Prussia?' And I suddenly

realized that I, just like everybody else, had an ethnic prejudice—
and it was deep-seated—from the World War II excitement we
had on the West Coast. We could almost imagine that we could go
out and kill and rape people. War allows everything, you see. Little
boys think that wars are absolutely the cat's meow. But I had not
been in the war, I had suffered nothing personally from the Germans
or the Prussians and, in any case, what the hell did I actually know
about Prussia? So that's how I became interested in it. Reading
about Prussia and the Baltic states, I found an extraordinary hodge-
podge of very powerfully held ethnic and national feelings. And
in the course of that I heard about Vamık Volkan who directs the
Center for the Study of Mind and Human Interaction at the
University of Virginia. His group had many years of experience
dealing with ethnic conflict. So I went to a conference—one of a
series—that Vamık and his colleagues were holding.

PETER HARCOURT: And it was Vamık who led you to the situation in
Estonia that you were to film in *The Dragon's Egg*?

ALLAN KING: That's right. Vamık's people were invited by Gorbachev's
people to go to the Baltic states and see if they could find some way
to make peace there, so that the Russians wouldn't get chucked out.
The principal problem to be dealt with was that Latvia and Estonia
especially, but also Lithuania, had very large numbers of Russian
speakers whom they feared and resented. There was a high risk that
the Soviet Union would not allow the Baltic states to achieve independence and, if they did, they might use the excuse of the persecution of former Soviet citizens to reinvade the Baltic states. It was a
highly volatile situation. A series of conferences were held, inviting
Estonians, Latvians, Lithuanians to meet over four or five days at a
time, in order to try and understand each other. And the Russians.
Vamık and his colleagues from the Center acted as facilitators.

Vamık had written an extraordinarily interesting book called
Bloodlines: From Ethnic Pride to Ethnic Terrorism [1997]. One part
of his theory suggested that all groups have a chosen trauma. And
the virtue of a trauma is that you can cherish it for generations. It
justifies some sort of recompense, something you are entitled to. It

also prevents people from mourning whatever trauma has occurred and moving on. Chosen trauma allows one to preserve hatred. It's similar to the tenacity with which individuals hold on to their key trauma. The greatest problem in reconciliation is to give up one's sense of injury sufficiently to allow oneself to hear one's opponent and try to put oneself in his or her position. Tough work if you've been occupied or been the occupier for centuries.

In the end, though, *The Dragon's Egg* isn't a tract about the exceptional work that Vamık Volkan's centre does. It's about how things worked out with the people he and his group were working with. It was an extraordinary experiment in democracy. Vamık and his group had finished their conference program by the time I had my film financed. So what we ended up filming was quite a different story.

The Center had been given three packets of $50,000 to give to each of three groups—at least ten Estonians and ten Russians in each, who could form a committee, agree on a goal, become incorporated, open a bank account and budget their project. Under the leadership of Olga Kamoshan, a remarkable half-Estonian, half-Russian woman, the people of Klooga, a smashed-up former Soviet army base, decided to build a community centre for their children. And by gosh, they did all these things, got their money. We end the film as they clean out a wrecked building and a truck carries off the debris. A year later we had the world premiere of the film in Klooga's newly completed and splendid community centre. Good luck or good fortune played a considerable part in their success, too.

In fact, Volkan, a brilliant psychoanalyst, was very frank about how many things are a matter of chance, despite

The Dragon's Egg

Aarne Irv
ESTONIAN COMMITTEE MEMBER

We've had parties here of up to 70 people.

The Dragon's Egg: Meeting Hall before   Meeting Hall after

what Freud says. And he is a Freudian. But he believes that many things in his life, the most important ones, were by chance, and it's the same for me. What you do with chance is another matter.

PETER HARCOURT: Was it hard to go back to documentary filmmaking?

ALLAN KING: Yes, I was a bit rusty. With *Dragon's Egg* I forgot to give the people as much time as I ought to have done so that they could really understand what it was we were doing. Not so much to understand the subject of the film—they knew that—but rather to get a feel for us. It took a while before they realized that we would be in their laps for a lot of time. We had to have a review meeting halfway through, when the people in the film wanted to go off on holidays. I pointed out that we were leaving at the end of June and it would be nice if they got to where they wanted to be on their project. So we did interfere a little, and I don't know if they would have got their building built when they got it built if we hadn't had that meeting. But I didn't tell them to build the building. I didn't tell them that it was about them achieving what they said their goal was. I just said it would be difficult filming if they were all on holidays and we weren't there.

BLAINE ALLAN: How much difference did it make to shoot *The Dragon's Egg* on digital video? When you made *Married Couple* it cost about $200,000 to shoot the seventy hours of 16mm film. How did that change?

ALLAN KING: *The Dragon's Egg* cost us $500,000 for a hundred hours of tape and six weeks' shooting. That's because all the other costs have gone up hugely. The money you save on digital cameras and digital tape is eaten back up again by the cost of the equipment that you use to digitize and make the transfers. The real virtue of digital stuff is that it is so portable. By the time that you get it on television it's fairly close to 16mm in quality but much, much quicker and easier to use. But the costs, proportionately, don't seem to have shifted all that much. Too much has been made of the change. A lot of it is really illusory.

BLAINE ALLAN: Tell us about your next film.

ALLAN KING: It's about following a number of people through the process of dying, burial and after. Getting into the research has been very slow because the whole business of privacy and confidentiality has been difficult to work through with the medical people in the hospitals. But if it's financed and we go ahead it will probably be at Sunnybrook [Hospital in Toronto]. I hope to be able to work in a reasonably bounded environment but one with some diversity in it. So that we start with a group of people, a place. And then over ten weeks or eight weeks, key figures will emerge with whom we can identify. So that's really what it's about. Because, I think, clearly there is nothing we fear more than dying. I don't know if there is any real way to come to terms with it other than playing at it, as it were, putting oneself into the experience in some emotionally vivid way, so one can come to terms with it.

SETH FELDMAN: Your other project, though, is going in the other direction, back to your beginnings. You are starting to write your memoirs. How did that get started?

ALLAN KING: It started actually when I was in analysis, in the 1970s. My analyst couldn't keep track of the various houses I'd lived in and schools I had gone to and he asked if I would just kindly write it down so he could get it straight. So I started and I went through the first six years of my life. After he got about sixty pages of it, he said, "Of course you're not going to publish this." And I was crushed. Of course I was going to publish it. I thought it was pure gold, you see.

So I stopped for thirty years. I started writing again earlier this year and gave myself an awful fright. I couldn't find the thread, and couldn't pick up the story. But I have got back into it and now I am up to 1939, going into grade five, my mother and father's second honeymoon. We went in a trailer, my father was selling cars by that time, and we went off to a trip to Grand Coulee Dam. By the end of the honeymoon I realized the marriage was again doomed. But we went through another year, grade five, which was the best year I ever had in school, actually.

BLAINE ALLAN: You also gave a paper to the Film Studies Association about making *Maria*. Was that part of your memoir?

ALLAN KING: No, but I did realize that I needed to write about my films. I was writing about them but it was all piecemeal. I had to get it all out and then I could find out what the shape might be. So that's why I'm writing now. But it's very difficult to make a living and find time to write. I've been totally absorbed in trying to get a masters' studio going for emerging documentarians. That would pay me some money. If I could write a book, that might pay me some money. And if I could get the film, that would pay me some money. Then I could afford to raise my son. But it's been tough going. I should go back to television episodes, though I don't know if I can either. Everyone likes young people in that business.

SETH FELDMAN: You said toward the beginning of this interview that filmmaking is about discovery. What have you discovered in all your films?

ALLAN KING: The disabusing thing is that you may learn a lot and indeed find a lot of answers, but you also find that there aren't any *real* answers and the world doesn't particularly get better—it gets different. But the difficulty of getting people to be peaceful or curb their greed and so on is the same as ever. I guess the gratification of getting older is that you know more about it and you become a little more equitable about it. And sometimes you can in fact do something effective. And some people *do* change.

Termini Station

Allan King:
Filmography

Compiled by Seth Feldman and Anne Doelman

Skidrow, 1956
38 min., 16mm, b&w
Production: CBC Vancouver
Screenplay: Ben Maartman
Narration: Art Hives
Photography: Jack V. Long
Editing: Arla Saare
Music: John Avison

The Yukoners, 1956
28 min., 16mm, b&w
Production: CBC Vancouver
Screenplay: Don Erickson
Narration: Art Hives
Photography: Jack V. Long
Editing: William Brayne
Music: Jerry Fuller

Portrait of a Harbour, 1957
28 min., 16mm, b&w
Production: CBC Vancouver
Screenplay: Jack V. Long, Jack Scott
Narration: George McLean
Photography: Bob Reid
Sound: Dave Pomeroy, Tom Mavrow,
    Ken Lowe
Editing: William Brayne, Jack Leyland
Music: John Avison

Gyppo Loggers, 1957
29 min., 16mm, b&w
Production: CBC Vancouver
Screenplay: Trevor Glucksman
Narration: Wally Marsh
Photography: John Seale
Editing: William Brayne

The Pemberton Valley, 1958
58 min., 16mm, b&w
Production: CBC Vancouver
Screenplay: George Robertson
Narration: George Robertson
Photography: Jack V. Long
Editing: Arla Saare
Music: Robert Turner

Where Will They Go?, 1959
28 min., 16mm, b&w
Production: Allan King Associates for
    Close-up (CBC)
Screenplay: George Robertson
Narration: George Robertson
Photography: Rolph Blakstad
Editing: William Brayne

Interviews for *Close-up*

In addition to documentary sequences, Allan King directed the following interviews for *Close-up*:

Brendan Behan, interviewed by Elaine Grand, 1959

Anthony Eden, interviewed by Blair Fraser, 1959

Orson Welles, interviewed by Bernard Braden, 1960

Jawaharlal Nehru, interviewed by Blair Fraser, 1960

Hewlett Johnson, interviewed by Douglas Leiterman, 1960

Arthur Koestler, interviewed by Elaine Grand, 1960

Peter Sellers, interviewed by Elaine Grand, 1960

Morris Schumaichter, interviewed by Blair Fraser, 1960

Lady [Kathleen] Epstein, interviewed by Elaine Grand, 1960

Frank Whittle, interviewed by Tom Hill, 1960

Thornton W. Burgess, interviewed by Bill Walker, 1960

Bullfight, 1960
18 min., 16mm, b&w
Production: Ross McLean for *Close-up* (CBC)
Screenplay: Robert Goldston
Narration: Frank Willis
Photography: Rolph Blakstad
Editing: Peter Moseley

India: Revolution by Consent, 1960
60 min., 16mm, b&w
Production: Douglas Leiterman
Screenplay: Douglas Leiterman for *Close-up* (CBC)
Narration: Blair Fraser

Photography: Rolph Blakstad
Sound: George Robertson

Rickshaw, 1960
28 min., 16mm, b&w
Production: Allan King Associates for *Close-up* (CBC)
Screenplay: George Robertson
Narration: George Robertson
Photography: Rolph Blakstad
Editing: Peter Moseley
Music: Indian Music Circle (London)
Other Title: *Rickshaw Boy*

A Matter of Pride, 1961
60 min., 16mm, b&w
Production: Ross McLean for *Close-up* (CBC)
Screenplay: Allan King
Narration: Frank Willis
Interviewer: Bob Quintrel
Photography: Jack Long
Editing: Helga Faust

Morocco, Land of the Atlas, 1961
58 min., 16mm, b&w
Production: Richard Ballentine for *Close-up* (CBC)
Screenplay: Clifford Irving
Narration: John Scott
Photography: Rolph Blakstad
Editing: William Brayne

Josef Drenters, 1961
30 min., 16mm, b&w
Production: Ross McLean for *Quest* (CBC)
Screenplay: Kyra Gordon
Narration: Andrew Allen
Photography: Peter Kelly
Editing: Michael Foytenyi
Music: Robert Turner, conducted by Louis Applebaum

Three Yugoslavian Portraits, 1961
30 min., 16mm, b&w
Production: Jim Guthro, Richard
Ballentine for *Close-up* (CBC)
Screenplay: Charles Fullman
Narration: Frank Willis
Photography: Rolph Blakstad, Robert
Crone
Editing: Noel Dodds
Supervised by: Richard Ballentine
Other Title: *Yugoslav Workers and
Marshall Tito*

Dreams, 1962
30 min., 16mm, b&w
Production: Allan King for *Quest* (CBC)
Screenplay: Allan King
Photography: Graham Woods
Editing: Noel Dodds
Cast: Ray Bonin, Sharon Younger

**The Pursuit of Happiness: Beyond
the Welfare State**, 1962
57 min., 16mm, b&w
Production: Douglas Leiterman for
Document (CBC)
Production: Allan King
Photography: Rolph Blakstad,
Richard Leiterman
Editing: Bruce Parsons
Music: Cornelius Cardew

Hamburg, Germany, 1963
30 min., 16mm, b&w
Production: Patrick Watson for
Inquiry (CBC)
Story: Roy Faibish
Photography: Richard Leiterman,
Robert Dutru
Editing: Bud Neate
Other Title: *Hamburg Show*

Le Grand Charles, 1963
30 min., 16mm, b&w
Production: John Kennedy for
Close-up (CBC)
Screenplay: Allan King
Narration: Frank Willis
Photography: Rolph Blakstad,
Richard Leiterman
Editing: Don Haig

Joshua: A Nigerian Portrait, 1963
57 min., 16mm, b&w
Production: Douglas Leiterman for
Document (CBC)
Screenplay: Wole Soyinka
Narration: Wole Soyinka
Photography: Rolph Blakstad
Editing: Bruce Parsons, Crea
Tarrant
Sound: Titus Adetogun

The Peacemakers, 1963
54 min., 16mm, b&w
Production: Douglas Leiterman for
Document (CBC)
Screenplay: Allan King
Narration: John Freeman
Photography: Richard Leiterman
Sound: Terry Cooke
Editing: William Brayne

The Field Day, 1963
12 min., 16mm, b&w
Production: Allan King Associates
Screenplay: Based on Kenneth Brown's
play *The Brig*
Photography: Richard Leiterman
Editing: William Brayne
Sound: Terrence Cooke
Cast: The Living Theatre

Our Dancing Export, 1964
26 min., 16mm, b&w
Production: Ross McLean for *Telescope*
(CBC)
Screenplay: Robert Goldston
Narration: Fletcher Markle
Photography: Richard Leiterman,
Colin Jones (stills)
Sound: Christian Wangler
Editing: William Brayne
Music: Matyas Seiber, Peter Racine
Fricker
Other Title: *Lynn Seymour: Portrait of
a Ballerina*

Horseman, Pass By, 1964
57 min., 16mm, b&w
Production: Dick Knowles for *Camera
Canada* (CBC)
Screenplay: Sean Mulcahy
Narration: Sean Mulcahy
Photography: Richard Leiterman
Sound: Tom Clarke

Bjorn's Inferno or The Devil to Pay,
1964
53 min., 16mm, b&w
Production: Douglas Leiterman for
Document (CBC), Allan King
Associates
Screenplay: Robert Goldston
Photography: Rolph Blakstad
Sound: Russell Heise
Editing: William Brayne
Cast: Barrie Simmons, Bjorn
Halversen, Fran Halversen

The Sound of Christopher Plummer,
1964
53 min., 16mm, b&w
Co-director: William Brayne
Production: Peter Kelly for *Telescope*
(CBC)

Interviewer: Fletcher Markle
Photography: William Brayne
Sound: Christian Wangler
Editing: William Brayne

**Running Away Backwards or
Coming of Age in Ibiza**, 1964
50 min., 16mm, b&w
Production: Allan King Associates for
the CBC
Screenplay: Robert Goldston
Photography: Richard Leiterman
Sound: Christian Wangler
Editing: Peter Moseley
Music: Cornelius Cardew
Cast: Richard Gardner, Richard
Suskind, Ginette Suskind, Mili
Newbury, Gisella Klapdor

The Most Unlikely Millionaire, 1965
27 min., 16mm, b&w
Production: Peter Kelly for *Telescope*
(CBC)
Screenplay: Allan King
Photography: Graham Woods
Sound: Gerry King
Editing: Kirk Jones

Warrendale, 1967
100 min., 16mm, b&w
Production: Patrick Watson and
George Desmond for the CBC
Photography: William Brayne
Sound: Russel Heise, Michael Billings
Editing: Peter Moseley

Children in Conflict, 1967
Eighteen 30-minute films edited from
footage taken during the filming of
Warrendale, including *School, A
Talk with Irene* and *Wake Up*.

Who Is James Jones?, 1968
30 min., 16mm, colour
Production: Allan King Associates for
Creative Persons, co-produced by
the CBC, BBC, PBS, Bayerische
Rundfunk
Screenplay: Peter Moseley
Photography: William Brayne
Sound: Ivan Sharrock
Editing: Peter Moseley

The New Woman, 1968
60 min., 16mm, colour
Production: CTV
Screenplay: Rita Greer Allen
Narration: Rita Greer Allen
Photography: Richard Leiterman
Editing: Arla Saare

A Married Couple, 1969
96 min., 16mm, colour
Production: Allan King Associates for
Aquarius Films Ltd.
Screenplay: Allan King
Photography: Richard Leiterman,
David Martin (assistant
cameraman)
Sound: Christian Wangler, Ron
Alexander (re-recording)
Editing: Arla Saare, Peter Rowe, Fred
Hillyer, Manuel Lumbreraz
Music: Zalman Yanofsky
Cast: Antoinette Edwards, Billy
Edwards, Bogart Edwards

**Mortimer Griffin, Shalinsky and
How They Settled the Jewish
Question**, 1971
30 min., 16mm, colour
Production: David Peddie for *To See
Ourselves* (CBC)
Screenplay: Michael John Nimchuck
from the story by Mordecai Richler

Photography: Edmund Ing Long
Editing: M. C. Manne
Sound: Eric Kettle
Music: Morris Surdin
Cast: Colin Fox, E. M. Margolese,
Daphne Gibson, James Edmond,
Susan Mainzer, Martin Lavut
Other Title: *Mortimer Griffin*

Can I Count You In?, 1972
30 min., 16mm, colour
Production: David Peddie for *To See
Ourselves* (CBC)
Screenplay: Patricia Watson from a
story by Shirley Faessler
Photography: Stanley Clinton
Editing: Eric Wrate
Cast: Jayne Eastwood, Cosette Lee,
Les Carlson, Sylvia Shawn, Peg
Secord

Delilah, 1972
30 min., 16mm, colour
Production: David Peddie for *To See
Ourselves* (CBC)
Screenplay: Brian Barney
Photography: Walter Wicks
Editing: Eric Wrate
Cast: Terry Tweed, Miles McNamara,
Jack Van Evera, Steve Pernie,
Barbara Hamilton, Ed McNamara,
Cy Mack

Come On Children, 1973
94 min., 16mm, colour
Production: Allan King Associates
Photography: William Brayne
Sound: Brian Avery
Editing: Arla Saare
Music: John Hamilton, Jack Zaza,
Alex Zivojinovich
Cast: John Hamilton, Lesley Henry,
Alex Zivojinovich, Ken Gibbs,

Noreen McCallum, Jo Ann Lye,
Richard McMullen, Alan
Dunikowski, Jane Harrison,
Sharon Wall

A Bird in the House, 1973
60 min., 16mm, colour
Production: Ronald Weyman for
Anthology (CBC)
Screenplay: Patricia Watson, based on
a story by Margaret Laurence
Photography: Ken Gregg
Cast: Paul Harding, Louise
Vallance, Wendy Thatcher, Pat
Hamilton, Nan Stewart, Henry
Stamper

Pity the Poor Piper, 1974
30 min., 16mm, colour
Production: David Peddie for *To See
Ourselves* (CBC)
Screenplay: Douglas O. Spettigue
Cast: Donald Davis, Bob Joy, Cosette
Lee

Last of the Four-Letter Words, 1975
60 min., 16mm, colour
Production: David Peddie for
Performance (CBC)
Screenplay: Nicka Rylski
Photography: Stanley Clinton
Editing: Myrtle Virgo
Cast: Jayne Eastwood, Les Carlson,
Phyllis Marshall, Linda Sorenson,
Pat Hamilton, Colin Fox

Baptizing, 1975
60 min., 16mm, colour
Production: David Peddie for
Performance (CBC)
Screenplay: Patricia Watson, adapted
from a chapter of *Lives of Girls and
Women* by Alice Munro

Photography: Edmund Long
Editing: Myrtle Virgo
Music: Ed Vincent
Cast: Jennifer Munro, Michael
McVarish, Robert Martyn, Wendy
Thatcher, Kay Hawtrey, Gerard
Parkes, Helen Hughes, Clare
Coulter

Six War Years, 1975
57 min., video, colour
Production: Robert Sherrin for
Performance (CBC)
Screenplay: Barry Broadfoot
Photography: Tom Farquharson,
Iamonn Beglan, Mike Gyll, Dave
Doherty
Editing: Leslie Brown
Cast: Blair Brown, Janet Amos, Claire
Coulter, Douglas McGrath, Ken
Pogue, Nick Mancuso, Thomas
Hauff, Miles Potter, Dominic
Hogan

Red Emma, 1976
60 min., 16mm, colour
Production: Allan King for
Performance (CBC)
Co-director: Martin Kinch
Screenplay: Carol Bolt from her play
Red Emma
Photography: Edmund Long
Editing: Arla Saare
Music: Phillip Schreibman
Cast: Chapelle Jaffe, Nick Mancuso,
Jim Henshaw, David Bolt, Brenda
Donohue, William Webster, Saul
Rubinek

Theatre in Canada, 1976
60 min., 16mm, colour
Production: Allan King Associates
Screenplay: Allan King

Featuring: Clips of theatre performances by Gordon Pinsent, Chapelle Jaffe, R.H. Thomson, Jayne Eastwood, Les Carlson

Maria, 1977
46 min., 16mm, b&w
Production: Stephen Patrick for *Here to Stay* (CBC)
Screenplay: Rick Salutin
Photography: Edmund Long
Cast: Diane D'Aquila, Enzina Berti, Jean Gascon, Alfie Scopp, Robert Silverman, Janet Amos, Booth Savage, Nancy Beatty

On the Job, 1977
57 min., video, colour
Co-director: Martin Kinch
Production: Robert Sherrin for *Performance* (CBC)
Screenplay: David Fennario
Photography: Tom Farquharson, Iamonn Beglan, Mike Gyll, George Clements
Music: Des McAnuff
Cast: R. H. Thomson, Thomas Hauff, Michael Rudder, Gerard Parkes, Yvan Canuel, Bob Silverman

Who Has Seen the Wind, 1977
101 min., 35mm, colour
Production: Allan King Associates
Screenplay: Patricia Watson from the novel by W. O. Mitchell
Photography: Richard Leiterman
Editing: Arla Saare
Music: Eldon Rathburn
Cast: Brian Painchaud, Gordon Pinsent, Helen Shaver, Chapelle Jaffe, Jose Ferrer, Charmion King, Patricia Hamilton

One Night Stand, 1978
93 min., 35mm, colour
Production: Allan King Associates for *Front Row Centre* (CBC)
Screenplay: Carol Bolt from her play *One Night Stand*
Photography: Ken Gregg
Sound: Erik Hoppe
Editing: Myrtle Virgo
Cast: Chapelle Jaffe, Brent Carver, Dinah Christie, Susan Hogan, Mina E. Mina, Len Doncheff, Robert Silverman, Pixie Bigelow, Don Daynard

Silence of the North, 1981
100 min., 35mm, colour
Production: Murray Shostak, Robert Baylis for Universal Films
Screenplay: Patricia Louisiana Knop
Photography: Richard Leiterman
Sound: Glenn Gauthier
Editing: Arla Saare, Eve Newman
Music: Allan Macmillan, Neil Young, Jerold Immel
Cast: Ellen Burstyn, Tom Skerritt, Gordon Pinsent

Ready for Slaughter, 1983
55 min., 16mm, colour
Production: Sig Gerber, Maryke McEwen for *For the Record* (CBC)
Screenplay: Roy MacGregor
Photography: Brian R. R. Hebb
Editing: Eric Wrate
Sound: Tom Bilenkey
Music: Milton Barnes
Cast: Gordon Pinsent, Diana Belshaw, Pat Cull, Layne Coleman, Booth Savage, J. Winston Carroll, Mavor Moore, Mina E. Mina, Jacqueline McLeod, James Ednud, Kevin Govier, Cecil Bridge

Who's in Charge?, 1983
118 min., video, colour
Production: Allan King
Direction: Sig Gerber
Photography: Eamonn Beglan, Tom Farquharson, Peter Brunson, Martin Kaiser, David Wright
Sound: Jules Bergeron
Editing: Eric Wrate
Cast: Conference Director: Gordon Lawrence
Consultants: Elie Debbane, MD, Gordon Lawrence, Austin Lee, MD
Participants: Peter Blackburn, Alex Busin, Syvie Carron, Jan Cervinka, Jane Crawley, André Daglis, Doris de Young, Shirley Dowell, Leo Foisy, Chuck Gauthier, H. L. Gosain, Gary Hanel, Julie Lariviere, Dave MacDougal, Gordon Morrisseau, Donna Mundell, Kim Neuman, Sandra Nichol, Emily North, Sam Organ, Bob Perry, Larry Provenzano, John Quarterly, Susan Robertson, Jack Sales, Ron St. Pierre, Donna L. Seguin, Mike Skinner, Bill Smith, Brad Wilson

The Last Season, 1987
60 min., 16mm, colour
Production: Robert Sherrin, CBC
Screenplay: Roy MacGregor based on his novel *The Last Season*
Photography: Vic Sarin
Sound: Dave Brown, Ter Malmberg
Editing: Ralph Brunjes
Music: Michael Conway Baker
Cast: Booth Savage, John Colicos, Neil Munro, Eric Peterson, Clare Coulter, Bernard Hopkins, Deborah Cass, David, Ferry, J. Winston Carroll, Johanna Raunio

Tucker and the Horsethief, 1985
45 min., 16mm, colour
Production: John Brunton for *Insight*
Screenplay: Mary Pleshette Willis
Cast: Sarah Boyd

Termini Station, 1989
107 min., 35mm, colour
Production: Don Haig, Douglas Leiterman, Allan King for *Saturday Plays*
Screenplay: Colleen Murphy
Photography: Brian R. R. Hebb
Sound: Peter Shewchuk
Editing: Gordon McClellan
Music: Mychael Danna
Cast: Megan Follows, Colleen Dewhurst, Gordon Clapp, Debra McGrath, Leon Pownall, Elliot Smith, Norma Dell'Agnese, Hannah Lee

Leonardo: A Dream of Flight, 1998
48 min., 16mm, colour
Production: David Devine, Richard Mozer
Screenplay: Raymond Storey
Photography: Rick Maguire
Editing: Gordon McClellan
Music: Fiachra Trench
Cast: Brent Carver, David Felton, Cedric Smith, Tom Melissis, Natascia Diaz, Brenda Bazinet, Leon Pownall, Craig Manley, Bruce Boreman, Pamela Santini, Muriel Costantini.

The Dragon's Egg: Making Peace on the Wreckage of the Twentieth Century, 1998
110 min., video, colour
Production: Allan King

Commissioning Editor: Rudy
Buttignol for TV Ontario
Photography: William Brayne
Sound: Derek Pert, John Hazen
Editing: Nick Hector
Music: Bill Thompson

Episodic Series Television

This Hour Has Seven Days
King contributed the following segments:

Program Title: Show #27
Segment Synopsis: King directs the
segment on Beryl Fox's film about
an unadoptable child.

Program Title: Show #33
Segment Synopsis: King interviews
British actress Rita Tushingham.

The Collaborators
60 min., 16mm, colour
"Kiss the World Goodbye" (1974)

Home Fires
video
"Unconditional Surrender" (1983)

Alfred Hitchcock Presents
30-min. episodes, 16mm, colour
Episode 30 "If the Shoe Fits" (1985)
Episode 33 "The Impatient Patient"
(1985)
Episode 35 "Specialty of the House"
(1985)
Episode 38 "World's Oldest Motive"
(1987)
Episode 39 "Deathmate" (1987)
Episode 42 "Prism" (1988)
Episode 45 "Killer Takes All" (1988)

Episode 50 "Murder Party" (1985)
Episode 52 "User Deadly" (1988)
Episode 64 "Survival of the Fittest"
(1988)
Episode 68 "A Murder in Mind"
(1988)

Danger Bay
30-min. episodes, 16mm, colour
Episode 22 "A Place for Ponga"
(1986)
Episode 61 "Roots and Wings"
(1987)
Episode 68 "Deep Trouble" (1987)
Episode 73 "The Only Way Up Is
Down" (1988)
Episode 81 "Something New" (1988)
Episode 83 "Second Honeymoon"
(1988)
Episode 80 "Stormy Weather" (1988)
Episode 90 "The Rally" (1987)
Episode 107 "High Ice" (1990)
Episode 123 "Looking Back" (1990)

Friday the 13th: The Series
30-min. episode, 16mm colour and
b&w
Episode 9 "Root of All Evil" (1987)

The Twilight Zone
30-min. episodes, 16mm, colour
"Dream Me a Life" (1988)

Philip Marlow, Private Eye
60-min. episode, 16mm, colour
"Blackmailers Don't Shoot" (1989)

Neon Rider
60-min. episode, 16mm colour
Episode 10 "You Can Run" (1990)

Lightning Force
60-min. episodes, 16mm, colour
   Episode 3 "Belfast Says No" (1991)
   Episode 4 "Smart Bullet" (1991)
   Episodes 7 & 8 "Fallout: Parts 1
      and 2" (1991)

Kurt Vonnegut's Monkey House
30-min. episode, 16mm colour
   Pilot 3: "All the King's Horses" (1991)
   Other Titles: *Monkey House,*
      Welcome to the Monkey House

Road to Avonlea
60-min. episodes, 16mm, colour
   Episode 19 "Old Quarrels, Old
      Love" (Sept. 29, 1991)
      (screenwriter)
   Episode 21 "Sea Ghost" (Jan. 20, 1991)
   Episode 23 "Dreamer of Dreams"
      (Feb. 3, 1991)
   Episode 30 "Felix and Blackie"
      (Jan. 19, 1992)
   Episode 31 "Facts and Fictions"
      ("Another Point of View") (1992)
   Episode 33 "A Dark and Stormy
      Night" (Feb. 23, 1992)
   Episode 59 "The Minister's Wife"
      (1994)
   Episode 65 "Otherwise Engaged"
      (1994)
   Episode 78 "Homecoming" (1995)
   Episode 81 "Davey and the
      Mermaid" (1996)
   Episode 82 "Woman of Importance"
      (1996)

By Way of the Stars
60-min. episodes, 16mm, colour
   Episode 1 (1993)
   Episode 2 (1993)
   Episode 3 (1993)
   Episode 4 (1993)

Ready or Not
30-min. episodes, 16mm, colour
   Episode 24 "Monkey See, Monkey
      Do" (1994)
   Episode 30 "Under One Roof"
      (1994)
   Episode 32 "Three's a Crowd" (1994)
   Episode 44 "I Do, I Don't" (1996)
   Episode 56 "Your Own Money"
      (1997)

Kung Fu: The Legend Continues
60-min. episodes, 16mm, colour
   Episode 33 "The Possessed" (1994)
   Episode 58 "The Promise" (1995)
   Episode 60 "Eye Witness" (1995)
   Episode 62 "Citizen Caine" (1995)
   Episode 64 "Kung Fu Blues" (1995)

Twice in a Lifetime
60-min. episodes, 16mm, colour
   Episode 2 "Death and Taxes" (1999)
   Episode 3 "The Healing Touch"
      (1999)
   Episode 8 "School's Out" (1999)
   Episode 12 "What She Did for Love"
      (1999)
   Episode 27 "My Blue Heaven"
      (2000)

Allan King on the set of
Who Has Seen the Wind

Selected
Bibliography

Writings by Allan King

King, Allan. "Notes on My Craft." In *An Allan King Retrospective* [unpaginated]. Montreal: La Cinémathèque canadienne, 1966 [pamphlet].

———. "The Coffee Boy Syndrome and Other Observations." *Journal of Canadian Studies* 16, no. 7 (Spring 1981): 82–89.

———. "The Forest from the Trees. *Cinema Canada*, no. 84 (May 1982): 34–37.

———. "Ironic Ethics: In the Mind of the Projector." *Cinema Canada*, no. 102 (December 1983): 22–23.

———. "More Muddy Morals: A Reply to Critics." *Cinema Canada*, no. 104 (February 1984): 6–7.

———. "*Pourquoi?* Round Two." *Cinema Canada*, no. 159 (January 1989): 5.

———. "The White Island: Coming of Age in Ibiza." *Montage* (Spring 2001): 36–37.

Writings about Allan King

An Allan King Retrospective. Montreal: La Cinémathèque canadienne, 1966. 30 leaves [unpaginated pamphlet].

Alpert, Hollis. "Suitable Cases for Treatment." *Saturday Review* 51, no. 39 (28 September 1968): 54.

Armstrong, Mary Ellen. "Tribute to Allan King: Truth, Fiction and the Issues in Between." *Playback* (13 January 1997): 14–19.

Block, Stephen. "The *Who's In Charge?* Debate—Conclusion: King of the Mixed-Media Metaphor." *Cinema Canada*, no. 107 (May 1984): 21–22.

Blumer, Ronald. *Take One* 2, no. 4 (March–April 1969): 22.

Callenbach, Ernest. "*Warrendale.*" *Film Quarterly* 21, no. 2 (Winter 1967–1968): 52–55.

Cobb, David. "Day of the Gopher." *Maclean's* 89, no. 19 (1 November 1976): 42, 44, 46, 48, 50–52, 54, 56.

"Conversations on Film with Allan King." *Canadian Cinematography* 4, no. 4 (May–June, 1965): 11–14.

Dawson, Jan. "*Warrendale.*" *Sight and Sound* 37, no. 1 (Winter 1967–1968): 44–46.

Dorland, Michael. "Pawns of Experience." *Cinema Canada*, no. 102 (December 1983): 23–24.

Harcourt, Peter. "A Celebration of People." *Cinema Canada*, no. 40 (September 1977): 22–29.

Harris, Christopher. "Still Harrowing after 30 Years: *Warrendale.*" *Globe and Mail* (22 January 1997): C1.

Hofsess, John. "Allan King." In *Inner Views: Ten Canadian Filmmakers*. Toronto: McGraw-Hill Ryerson, 1975, 55–65.

———. "Allan King Ends the Sixties: Everybody Waved Goodbye." *Maclean's* 84, no. 3 (March 1972): 86.

———. "Hard Faith for Hard Times." *Canadian* (25 December 1976): 12–15.

Jackson, David. "Warrendale." *Canadian Forum* 47 (July 1967): 77–78.

Kael, Pauline. "The Current Cinema: Trends and Paroxysms." *New Yorker* (14 February 1970): 114–18.

Kaufmann, Stanley. "Children of Our Time." *New Republic* 159, no. 12 (21 September 1968): 24, 41–42.

Klady, Len. "Oh! For a Little Southern Comfort." *Cinema Canada*, no. 64 (April 1980): 25–28.

Martin, Bruce. *Allan King: An Interview with Bruce Martin and a Filmography.* Edited by Alison Reid. Ottawa: Canadian Film Archives, 1970.

Michener, Wendy. "The Brilliant Canadian Film You Can't See." *Maclean's* 80, no. 7 (July 1967): 6.

Pratley, Gerald. "In Conversation with Director Allan King: *Who Has Seen the Wind*." *Showbill* (October–November 1977): 34–35.

———. "The National Film Board of Canada: Then and Now (Part 3)." *Kinema*, 17 (Spring 2002): 5–16.

Rolfe, Lee. "Visiting Arcola." *Cinema Canada*, no. 33 (December 1976–January 1977): 29–32.

Robertson, George. "Perverse Misreadings." *Cinema Canada*, no. 104 (February 1984): 7.

Rosenthal, Alan. "*A Married Couple.*" In *The New Documentary in Action: A Casebook in Film Making*, 21–65. Berkeley, California: University of California Press, 1971.

Saunders, Doug. "Vérité Vision: He Likes to Listen." *Globe and Mail*, 31 March 1999.

Stiles, Mark. "Allan King, Film Director." *Cinema Papers*, no. 30 (December 1980–January 1981): 436–48.

Tadros, Connie. "Two Directors Look at Pay TV." *Cinema Canada*, no. 78 (October 1981): 25–27.

Watson, Patrick. *Notes on Warrendale*. Toronto: Canadian Broadcasting Corporation, (1967) [pamphlet].

Acknowledgements

It was Piers Handling and Steve Gravestock of the Toronto International Film Festival who decided that an Allan King retrospective was long overdue. This book, which accompanies the retrospective, was produced under the guidance of Catherine Yolles who brought her usual finesse to the task. She was expertly assisted in her editing tasks by Doris Cowan, and the book was designed by the accomplished Gordon Robertson.

The Canada Council for the Arts provided generous financial support for this publication.

Special thanks to the Canadian Broadcasting Corporation for its assistance in preparing and restoring prints and videotapes for the Allan King retrospective at the 2002 Toronto International Film Festival. This project was completed with the contributions of John Hazen, Russ McMillen, Jay Mowat, Laurie Nemetz, Harold Redekopp and Laurie Wilhelm.

Allan King's long and complex career could not have been documented without the boundless energies of Peter Harcourt and Blaine Allan, and my graduate assistant Anne Doelman (a.k.a. Wonder GA). This book also owes much to the assistance of Anne Goddard and Jean Matheson (National Archives of Canada) as well as Sylvia Frank, Robin MacDonald, Eve Goldin and Hubert Toh (The Film Reference Library). Thanks must also go to Stacey Hertzman and Sarah Zammit, at Allan King Associates, and to Allan's long time friend, Stan Fox. And, of course, it is Allan King who deserves our most profound gratitude, not only for the amount of time and thought he has contributed to this book, but also for his lifetime of achievement.

Seth Feldman

Text and Illustration Sources

Text Sources

"Allan King: A Celebration of People" by Peter Harcourt was written for *The Human Elements* (Oberon, 1978), edited by David Helwig, and first appeared in *Cinema Canada* 40 (September 1977). It was included in *Take Two: A Tribute to Film in Canada* (Irwin, 1984), edited by Seth Feldman, and revised for this publication. Copyright © Peter Harcourt 1978, 2002.

Illustration Sources

Title page photograph of Allan King copyright © Ben Mark Holzberg.

Film stills are courtesy of The Film Reference Library, Toronto, The National Archives of Canada and Allan King Associates. All film stills and documents (excluding Lindsay Anderson's *Thursday's Children*), unless otherwise noted, copyright © Allan King Associates, Toronto. Stills from the National Archives of Canada / PA212190 / PA212191 / PA21292 copyright © Allan King Associates and Robert A. Ritchie. National Archives of Canada / PA212194 copyright © Allan King Associates and the Canadian Broadcasting Corporation.

Special thanks to Peter Harcourt for his research of the film stills.